Old English Paperweights

Robert G. Hall

Schiffer Publishing Ltd

4880 Lower Valley Rd. Atglen, PA 19310 USA

Dedication

This book is dedicated to my wife Eileen, for taking over my chores in the house and garden to enable me to write this book and for being my confidante and supporter for thirty-five years.

Hall, Robert, 1943`
Old English paperweights / Robert Hall.
p. cm.
Includes bibliographical references and index.
ISBN 0-7643-0539-5 (hardcover)
1. Paperweights--England--Catalogs. I. Title.
NK5440.P3H34 1998
748.8'4'0942075--dc21

Designed by Laurie A. Smucker
Typeset in *Lydian Cursive BT*/*Korinna BT*

ISBN: 0-7643-0539-5
Printed in China
1 2 3 4

Published by Schiffer Publishing Ltd.
4880 Lower Valley Road
Atglen, PA 19310
Phone: (610) 593-1777; Fax: (610) 593-2002
E-mail: Schifferbk@aol.com
Please write for a free catalog.
This book may be purchased from the publisher.
Please include $3.95 for shipping.

In Europe, Schiffer books are distributed by
Bushwood Books
6 Marksbury Avenue
Kew Gardens
Surrey TW9 4JF England
Phone: 44 (0)181 392-8585; Fax: 44 (0)181 392-9876
E-mail: Bushwd@aol.com

Please try your bookstore first.

We are interested in hearing from authors with book ideas on related subjects.

Contents

Acknowledgments

This book would not have been the same without the contributions of many people, but my special thanks go to the following in particular:

my eldest son Richard, who got me started with the word processor
my youngest son Peter, who runs my business, allowing me the time to write this book
Andy Barbaro, who has shown me the way on the computer.

My thanks to the following people who have all made the writing of this book a little easier than trying to do it alone. Their help with photos and advice was invaluable.

Julian Arculus
Alfred Noel Arculus
Tom Guy Arculus
Roger Dodsworth
Gerald Ball
Neal Robinson
Anne Anderson
Colin McCallien
Terry and Hilary Johnson
Roy Brown
Bill and Marge Volkman
Simon Marshall
Karen & Paul Dunlop
Mr. & Mrs. Richard Giles
Simon Williams
Sam Thompson
Mr. Skidmore
Dr. Geoffrey Dutton
Portia Gallery
Anne Metcalfe.(Sweetbriar Gallery)
Margaret Preston
Marlene Van Horne White
Joan Pettifor
Gilbert Hill
Bergstrom Mahler Museum
Eric Reynolds

Introduction

Paperweight collecting eventually becomes a little obsessive with most collectors, and it seems that we all travel the same road in our quest for the rarest and most beautiful weights. From that first seemingly innocuous purchase of a pretty and unusual object encased in glass, we develop the need to find out "where it was made" from a reference book in the local library, which then opens the door to the immense variety of colors, canes, and subjects to be found in these fascinating glass baubles. The problem with trying to identify any English paperweights you many encounter is the sparse and fragmented information found in books on paperweights, usually only one or two pages with few photographs. Virtually every book written on paperweights will contain some information on English weights, but the inconvenience of having to wade through five or six books trying to find an answer can be quite frustrating, especially as new evidence, points of view, and debate are surfacing on a regular basis through collector organizations and magazines. It was for this reason that I decided to try gathering into the same book all of the known information that was still relevant, together with as many photographs as possible of English weights having both known and unknown attributions. Seeing these unknown but obviously English weights can also aid the collector and encourage more research into this subject. The more we see and read about our chosen subject, the more we need to know, the more our thirst for information is unquenchable.

Many collectors have acquired as many books and auction catalogues on the subject as they have paperweights, and with the knowledge gained from books a new collector can venture forth in the hunt for that first "big buy." This may lead you to the local antique fairs or auction house, where your first tentative step could be fraught with danger. The bargain you have just purchased from a seemingly knowledgeable general dealer in antiquities or an auction house that specializes in house clearances may well turn out to be the genuine article, but is more likely a 1930s copy. It is only with experience, and by seeing and handling paperweights, that we begin to understand the complex world of paperweight collecting. When you do make that initial "bargain buy," however, you will find yourself bitten by the bug. You may be unsure at first, but when you get home and confirm, in your catalogue or book, that it is indeed a Bacchus or Clichy antique, and you only paid $150 for it, there will be no holding you back. Every weekend you will be found searching the flea markets and antique fairs in a never-ending quest for rarer and more beautiful specimens. Once hooked, you will eventually build your collection from auction houses and specialist dealers knowledgeable in this art form.

The search for paperweights made in the period between 1845 and 1852 can be a long road to take, however. Referred to as the "classic period," this was a time when paperweights and other millefiori objects were made by the thousands in France and Bohemia. Although many were made, the very nature of glass meant that only a relative few would survive to the present day. It is this rarity, as well as the collecting of antiques in general, that has made the paperweight such a prized and expensive item today. Many collectors may find that antique weights are outside their budgets, and may collect modern weights of collector quality instead. These will eventually appreciate in value and become "tomorrow's antiques," but this does not stop the hunt for the antique weights, a hunt which can be the most rewarding of pastimes.

English paperweights made in the classic period by George Bacchus and Islington Glassworks are the rarest of all paperweights, possibly produced only in the hundreds, rather than the thousands characteristic of their French and Bohemian counterparts. The French were masters at including all manner of subjects in their weights, including flowers, animals, snakes, and lizards. Much research has been done into the French makers, who left us with a reasonable amount of documentary evidence to authenticate their products. This research is aided by the fact that the two biggest French producers of paperweights are still in existence, namely Baccarat and Saint Louis. Both glasshouses have examples of their work from the 1840s. The English makers were not so benevolent, leaving virtually no evidence of paperweight making at all. This state of affairs probably arose because the market in paperweights went into a dramatic decline after 1852. As with many innovative but gimmicky products, everyone wants one for a few years but they can soon go out of fashion. It may have been that the English began making these millefiori products at the end of the paperweight's popularity, so only a few were made. This theory may also explain why the English only made millefiori concentrics, and never used lampworked flowers or animals. The lampworking techniques would have been a natural progression in the skills needed to produce paperweights in this style, but with the collapse of the market the English just did not have enough time to develop the skills required. Although the English weights were almost exclusively concentrics there is enough variety in the cane colors and composition to keep the collector interested.

So where were the first English millefiori paperweights made? This honour may rest with a Frenchman named George Bontemps, who came to England in 1848 from the Choisy-le-Rois glassworks near Paris. Bontemps began working for an English glassworks in Birmingham called Chance Brothers. The Choisy factory he had just left had been experimenting with millefiori paperweights until it closed in 1851. Chance Brothers were a very large glassworks specializing in commercial, optical, and plate glass, and so far no evidence has been found in the well-documented history of this factory that shows or mentions millefiori or paperweights. It may be that Bontemps passed on the secret of paperweight making at one of the monthly meetings attended by most of the local glassmakers. These meetings were held at a local hostelry to fix the price of labour and products for the next month. This was a common practice at the time, and cooperation between glassworks made sense for all concerned. A united front against foreign competition was encouraged by the larger firms, and the passing on of small pieces of business with production runs and markets too small to concern the big commercial producers could help smaller businesses such as Bacchus, Islington, and others, while also preventing price wars and undercutting. Evidence of this practice exists in the private diaries of the owners of the Stevens and Williams glassworks (1776-1930). These diaries are held at the Brierley Hill Glassworks Museum. This may only be theory and conjecture, but would also seem plausible given the circumstances.

The lack of hard evidence in the form of dated and signed millefiori paperweights leaves the researcher frustrated with the producers of these wonderful pieces of art. Had they only known and appreciated these "glass jewels" a little more, and treated them with the respect they are given today by signing and dating the better pieces, the task of identifying the unmarked weights by the matching of canes would be a simple task. I have used logic, conjecture, and my twenty-five years of experience collecting paperweights to bring about an order to the English paperweight. As this is the first book dedicated solely to understanding and identifying English paperweights, I hope this will lead to works by other researchers who may specialize even further, perhaps taking on one of the many glasshouses that flourished in the mid-nineteenth century and looking at it in minute detail. The task is daunting, but here is the start.

About the Price Guide

All prices quoted in this book are based on 1998 approximate values. Since most of the Bacchus paperweights have been in private collections for quite some time with hardly any appearing at auction in the last ten years, I have used the known values of recent auction prices coupled with the guidance of the owners. Prices are for pieces found to be in good condition. The author accepts no responsibility for paperweights and related items that may sell for more or less than the suggested value in this book.

Chapter One

The Making of a Millefiori Paperweight

After the canes are made and cut to length, the sized canes are placed in a ring mould made from steel or cast iron (Figure 1). It is at this stage that a loosely packed mould will cause the final paperweight to look untidy, so it is essential that canes are matched for size. Where necessary, small pieces of clear glass can be wedged in to prevent slippage occurring. The completed rings of canes are known as the "set-up".

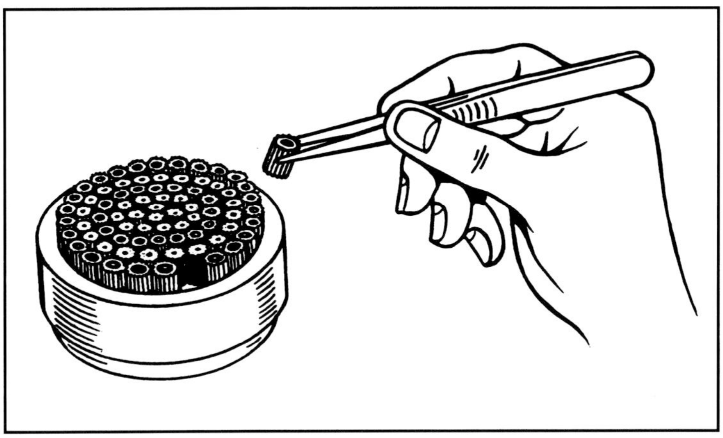

Figure 1

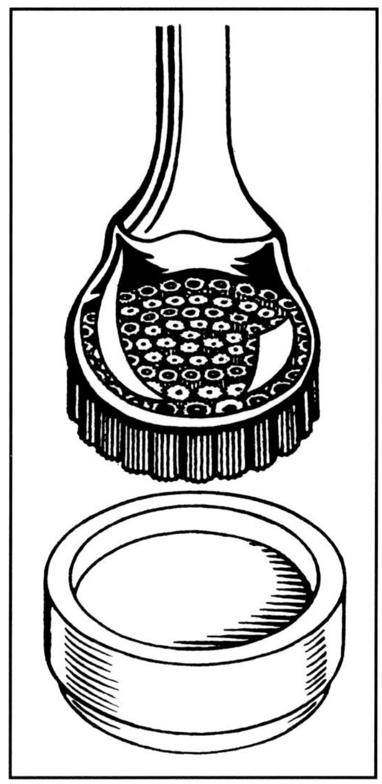

Figure 2

The second stage in the production of a paperweight is the picking up of the set-up by a gather of soft glass which has been collected from a furnace of molten glass on the end of a steel rod known as "the pontil." This glass is allowed to slowly fall in a controlled manner onto the set-up of canes. After waiting a few seconds to allow the glass to descend between the canes and to cool sufficiently, the set-up can be lifted from the ring mould by the pontil rod without disturbing the rows of canes (Figure 2). The cane set-up is then returned to the furnace where the final gather of glass to form the dome is collected.

With the paperweight almost complete, the weight is sized in a wooden mould and any excess glass is removed by cutting with shears (Figure 3). The rounding and shaping process may necessitate repeated trips to the "glory hole," which is the entrance aperture of the furnace. The paperweight is held in the glory hole on the end of the pontil rod, which is repeatedly turned to prevent the weight from falling off and into the furnace. After shaping, the paperweight is polished with the use of wet newspaper held flat on the hand and repeatedly wetted to prevent burning.

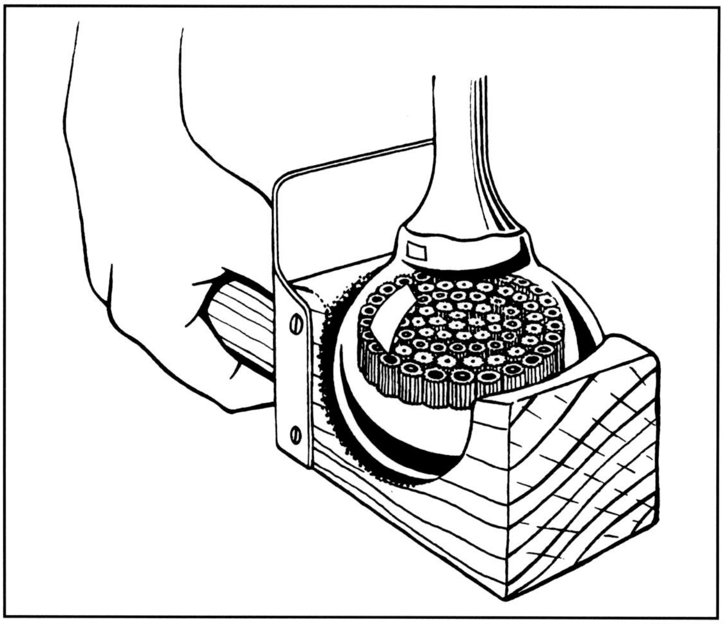

Figure 3

The final stage is the removal of the paperweight from the end of the pontil rod. This is done by directing a jet of air through a tube, onto the narrow part where the pontil joins the paperweight. This cools the weight sufficiently to allow a sharp tap on the pontil to detach the weight, which is allowed to fall onto wet newspaper or some other fireproof material. The finished paperweight is then placed in the annealing oven, which slowly reduces in temperature to prevent stress fractures in the finished weight. This process usually takes at least twelve hours or overnight to accomplish.

Once cool, the sharp pontil mark on the base can be removed by grinding and any facets cut. A final polish on the very fine abrasive wheel will remove any detritus on the surface.

The finished product.

Chapter Two

Sulphides by Apsley Pellat and Other English Makers

Apsley Pellatt (1791-1863) was a glass manufacturer in the 1820s and a great innovator of glass products and techniques. He developed a style and patent to encase a mixture of China clay and silicate of potash into glass. This paste could be either moulded or carved into any shape and design required. These moulded designs are now known as "sulphides."

The discovery of the technique for making moulded portraits goes to a sculptor from Scotland, James Tassie (1735-1799). He developed a business making these cameos and intaglio pieces for Josiah Wedgwood, the pottery manufacturers of Stoke on Trent, England. He also made paste "gems" for decorating glass and ornaments. Many of these sulphide inclusions were portraits of well-known and historical figures; Queen Victoria and Prince Albert, George Washington, and Napoleon were all popular subjects. They were included in many glass items, such as vases, mantle ornaments, decanters, and wine glasses, and also paperweights.

Apsley Pellatt may have been one of the first makers of paperweights. In the 1820s he had knowledge of the Venetian millefiori techniques, and went on to publish books on the subject of glass making. His *Memoir on the Origins of Glassmaking* describes how any ornament made from his ceramic paste could be included in glass without fracturing, as long as the fusion temperature of the piece is higher than that of the glass in which it is to be included. The method used for these inclusions is usually the complete covering of the ceramic moulding by molten glass, or alternatively by the insertion of the piece into a blown bubble of glass which is then collapsed by sucking out the trapped air within. These can then be used to decorate the sides of vases etc. Pellatt's technique for paperweights was to encase the usually white medallion in a crown of glass. Although he knew the millefiori techniques, he never used canes in any of the few paperweights that can be attributed to his glasshouse. Several pieces are known which have both millefiori canes and a sulphide inclusion and may be of English origin.

Queen Victoria Sulphide. Height 2". Dia. 2.75". $400-500. ***Courtesy of Mr. & Mrs. Richard Giles.***

A fine "Young Head" of the Queen, as she would be around the 1850s. These sulphides were very popular around the time of the Great Exhibition of 1851 and were probably sold in considerable numbers at the exhibition itself. Most large English glassmakers would have taken a stand at this showroom of the world's industry. Apsley Pellatt would have almost certainly had small items of glass for sale to the general public, at a time when paperweights were extremely popular items as gifts. As these pieces were hardly ever signed, the attribution to Pellatt can only be tentative. Many other makers were producing sulphides at the same time.

Prince Albert Sulphide. Height 2". Dia 2.75". $400-500. ***Courtesy of Mr. & Mrs. Richard Giles.***

The Queen and Prince Albert were regular visitors to the Great Exhibition. They were given many gifts by the exhibitors, and it was probably from these visits that the Royal collection of paperweights was begun.

The French manufacturers Clichy and Baccarat were the main producers of paperweights with sulphides and millefiori canes included, and other producers from Bohemia, Scotland, and England have been making sulphides throughout the nineteenth and twentieth centuries.

Apsley Pellatt exhibited at the 1851 Great Exhibition in London, winning high praise for "the whiteness and clarity" of his crystal. Many English glass houses have been credited with producing paperweights in the nineteenth century that have sulphide inclusions, but examples are extremely rare and elusive. As was normal with the English factories, very few were signed or can be attributed with any certainty.

One company which did sign their weights was Allen & Moore. Paperweights were sold showing the Crystal Palace building which housed the Great Exhibition of 1851, however Allen & Moore did not have a glassworks and probably had these items made for them by another glassworks. They were then sold as souvenirs at the Great Exhibition to a willing public eager to commemorate and remember this fantastic architectural masterpiece of the age. Allen & Moore, based in London, is listed in *Kellys Business Directory of 1854* as being "manufacturers of fancy goods" which did not include glass in its listing.

Two Birmingham companies were also involved in the manufacturing of sulphide type paperweights. These had the designs impressed "intaglio" into the bases of the weights, which were then dipped into an acid solution to leave the impression matt and visible through the dome of the weight. These weights could also be made of pressed glass or highly decorated with faceting. The Birmingham companies known to be involved in this technique were Oslers and Lloyd & Summerfield.

William Shakespeare Sulphide. Height 1.7". Dia. 2.7". $300-450. ***Author's Collection.***

This profile of Shakespeare shows how well made these sulphide medallions were. The crisp outline of the features and hair does credit to the artist craftsmen of the day. The bases of these sulphides followed the French fashion of removing the pontil by lightly grinding a concavity, leaving a 0.25 inch basal ring. This paperweight was identified as Pellatt since a vase and scent bottle known to be by him has the same bust included on the outside, as decoration.

Lord Nelson Sulphide. Height 2.75". Dia 2.25". $300-450. *Courtesy of Mr. & Mrs. Richard Giles.*

This paperweight has a distinctly different profile than the pieces attributed to Apsley Pellatt. The sulphide bust of Admiral Lord Nelson sits on the bottom of the glass dome which is almost egg shaped in construction. This paperweight has been attributed to the Scottish maker John Ford. Ford was based in Edinburgh in the 1870s.

Intaglio Lion Head Paperweight, Unknown Maker. Height 2.25". Dia. 2.6". $250-350. *Courtesy of Margaret Preston.*

This pressed glass intaglio paperweight does not quite seem to fit in the paperweight theme, until you actually pick up the piece and realize that it has all the attributes of a standard paperweight. Although it looks flat, it is in fact as tall as the average weight, with a tall dome of glass set on the intaglio base. The crystal dome is sparklingly clear and gives the paperweight an almost optical look. These intaglio pieces were made by many glasshouses, but in particular by Lloyd & Summerfield and F. & C. Osler, both of Birmingham. Paperweights were also made in the USA with the motif impressed into the base and a paperweight shaped dome on top.

Sulphide of Disraeli (1804-88). Height 2.75". Dia. 2.25". $300-400. *Courtesy of Mr. & Mrs. Richard Giles.*

This sulphide of the English Prime Minister Benjamin Disraeli is the same shape and size as the Lord Nelson sulphide.

Sulphide by Allen & Moore. Height 1.25". Dia. 2". $250-350. *Author's Collection.*

A small commemorative paperweight produced for the 1851 Great Exhibition. The sulphide tablet is encased in a small dome of clear glass and signed A.& M. LONDON 1851. The tablet is finely carved and very detailed for such a small piece of work. The magnifying property of the glass dome enhances the size. The wording around the edge reads: THE BUILDING OF THE INTERNATIONAL EXHIBITION.

Magnum Sulphide with Millefiori Canes. Dia. 3.75". *Courtesy of The Broadfield House Glass Museum, Kingswinford, England.*

A magnificent concentric and sulphide magnum by an unknown maker. The sulphide plaque is circled by three rows of precise cross canes and tubes in red and white, and blue and white. The tube canes are white with red centres, appearing to be hollow but filled with clear glass. A paperweight of this quality would have been made by a large and reputable glasshouse. The subject, The Earl William Wentworth Fitzwilliam (1748-1833), was an important dignitary who became Lord Lieutenant of Ireland for a short time, and any commemorative piece such as this would have been commissioned from a well known glassworks of the time. The sulphide medallion is signed WILSON, which would refer to John Wilson who was a maker of sulphide medallions in the latter part of the eighteenth century. Wilson did not make glass, although he would have had access to many glasshouses to which he sold his portraits and cameo gems, made from a vitreous enamel mix for inclusion in vases and other ornaments. The maker of the paperweight may never be known, but whoever was responsible did a fine job. It would be reasonable to assume that this piece would have been made during the lifetime of Earl Fitzwilliam, as no birth or death date appears. This would make this piece the earliest English millefiori paperweight known. The simple but beautiful canes in this weight could have been made in Venice or Bohemia or the whole weight could even have been commissioned abroad, but for one off piece or small order it would hardly seem worth the effort involved, and was probably made in England. The sulphide itself has an unusual feature: the surface has been coated with a material that has created thousands of minute bubbles, giving the sulphide a golden hue. The Earl Fitzwilliam had a colorful history, having been left the amazing fortune of £40,000 per year by his uncle the Lord Rockingham. He went into politics and became Lord Lieutenant of Ireland in 1794. His time in Ireland was very short-lived due to a political misunderstanding. Upon his arrival on Irish soil, he promptly dismissed the Commissioner for Customs, the Attorney, the Solicitor General, and the Secretary to the Military. The English Government refused to accept these dismissals and reinstated the men immediately. With this rebuff, Fitzwilliam resigned after less than one hundred days in office. Fitzwilliam appealed to both houses of parliament but was rejected by a large majority. Beresford, the dismissed commissioner for the Customs, then challenged Fitzwilliam to a duel. This challenge led to a meeting on the Tyburn Turnpike on the 26th June 1795 but the duel was halted by the arrival of the Constables. Fitzwilliam eventually made his peace with the Government and later became Lord Lieutenant of the West Riding of Yorkshire from 1798 to 1819, when he was dismissed from public office for using violent language at a public meeting.

Profile of Earl Fitzwilliam Paperweight. Height 1.75".

This profile shows a low dome, with the edges slightly under the weight. The strong colors to the canes can be seen clearly, the deep blue contrasting with the neighbouring red and white tubes. The cane ends, although set neatly in the weight, have not been cut to a precise length, but this does not detract from the overall construction of this important paperweight.

Base of Earl Fitzwilliam Paperweight.

The base is perfectly flat, showing a good amount of wear across the whole base. Islington Glassworks may be a contender for the attribution of this weight if it was indeed made in England. Of the three signed IGW known paperweights, at least one has a perfectly flat base. The other quality glass and paperweight maker of the period, Bacchus, drew their generally pastel colored canes under the weights and left a concave base and a quite wide ring around the edges. Islington also used strongly colored canes in their weights. The words on the base read:

HEIR TO
THE VIRTUES
AS WELL AS TO THE ESTATES
OF HIS UNCLE
CHARLES,
MARQUIS OF ROCKINGHAM
AND NOT MORE NEARLY ALLIED TO HIM
BY PROXIMITY OF BLOOD THAN BY
SIMILARITY OF MANNERS
HE GOVERNED IRELAND IN PEACE AD
1795, AND WAS LORD LIEUTENANT
OF THE WEST - RIDING OF YORKSHIRE FROM
1798 TO 1819

This paperweight is possibly unique and in remarkably good condition, and would be a star addition to any collection of paperweights.

Scent Bottle with Sulphide Decoration. Height 3". $850-1000. *Courtesy of Anne Anderson.*

A crystal scent bottle by Apsley Pellatt, with the sulphide portrait of William Shakespeare encased on the side of the bottle. This piece was probably made around 1820-30, at a time when the addition of sulphides to decorate vases and glasswares was at its most popular. With the arrival of millefiori, sulphide paperweights proved to be less saleable, with only a few made in comparison to the many thousands of millefiori and lampworked pieces produced around the 1850s. This portrait of Shakespeare can also be seen on a paperweight in this chapter, with the same sulphide tablet inclusion as used in this bottle.

Duke of Wellington Paperweight. Height 1.75". Dia. 2.5". $600-700. *Courtesy of Anne Anderson.*

A paperweight by Apsley Pellatt with a good likeness of the Duke of Wellington. The majority of paperweights produced by Apsley Pellatt would have featured classical portraits and many of the aristocracy and celebrities of his day. Although Pellatt knew of the millefiori technique, it was left to the French Baccarat and Clichy glassworks to combine sulphides and millefiori in the same weights on a production basis. Although it would be likely that he tried the process of combining the two, no known pieces exist to date.

Chapter Three

George Bacchus and Son

Union Glass Works, Dartmouth Street, Birmingham.

George Bacchus started his glass works with two partners, the Messrs. Green and Green, in 1818. That year they were mentioned in the Birmingham business directory *Kellys Post Office Address Book* as Bacchus Green and Green.

The name of the company was changed in 1833 to George Bacchus & Co. Although George died in 1840, the company prospered under the management of his son John. In 1841 the company was renamed George Bacchus & Son to recognize John, and changed again to George Bacchus & Sons in 1858. In 1860 the company was taken over by Stone, Fawdrey & Stone, however the Bacchus name was kept alive until the 1890s.

The Birmingham area in the early nineteenth century was a major producer of domestic and plateglass. With the removal of the last remaining sixpence per pound of the Glass Tax in 1845, the area began to recover business lost to the foreign producers from France and Bohemia. Birmingham glasshouses, along with the neighbouring area of Stourbridge only ten miles away, flourished without the burden of the tax and expanded the range of glassware they produced to incorporate "fancy glass in the Venetian style."

By 1848 Bacchus had begun to produce paperweights and exhibited their "letter weights" at the Society of Arts exhibition of 1849, held at the newly erected Bingley Hall Exhibition Centre in Birmingham. Their products on display drew excited comments from the Journal of Design & Manufacturing, "the specimens we have seen of the work on display are quite the equal in transparency, color, ingenuity and arrangement of the parts to the foreign work which stationers and fancy shops have been and are so crowded."

It would seem that the production of paperweights by Bacchus was quite small and although they also exhibited at the Great Exhibition of 1851 at the Crystal Palace in London, no mention was made of paperweights by name. However, the factory was awarded a prize medal for its glasswares.

Compared to the output of the French glass works of Clichy, Baccarat, and St. Louis, the Bacchus production was very limited, possibly only four hundred or so in total. The chance of discovering an unknown Bacchus weight is extremely small. Occasionally one will surface at an auction house and will be contested vigorously by collectors. The prices have been increasing steadily over the past few years, and auction prices for a good concentric in 1997 would be $3500 to $5000. Even weights with bruising and scratches will achieve nearly as much. These prices highlight the rarity of Bacchus weights. Searching through the old auction catalogues of the last ten years or so, only a handful of Bacchus weights have been sold compared to the many hundreds of French paperweights.

Bacchus produced several types of weights, including concentric, close packs, mushrooms, carpet grounds, overlays, baskets, and spaced concentrics. Some are faceted and others can have the canes pressed into a ground described as "sodden snow."

Sizes tend to be large, 3.25 inches or magnum 3.5 inches. There are exceptions but these two sizes are the most likely. The profiles of Bacchus weights have a crown of glass that appears lower than that of their French counterparts. The pin cushion shape of the cane set-up rises about half-way into the dome, and when viewed from above appears to completely fill the weight to capacity.

The pontil mark is normally removed by hollow grinding to leave a shallow concavity, and the base will usually show a wide basal ring of 0.25 to 0.5 inches.

The colors of Bacchus canes have been described as "pallid" and "muted" pastels, but occasionally one will be seen with deep blues and reds. The variety and complexity of the canes and the arrangements more than make up for the lack of color depth of the canes. Some very unusual colors have appeared in several Bacchus paperweights, including pale fluorescent green, lilacs and lavenders, pistachio green, and pale yellow. The blending of the pastel colors has been arranged very sympathetically in most cases, with the colors gently drifting into and not contrasting with their neighbours.

Two Early Bacchus Concentrics, c. 1850. ***Courtesy of Bill Volkman.***

The sizes of these two very similar weights are, on the left: Height 2.3". Dia. 3.1". with a value of $2750-3250; and on the right: Height 2.4". Dia. 3.3" with a value of $2000-2500. The cane set-ups are almost identical, with the row of green and white ruffle canes from the same cane rod. But the difference in the way the canes end in the outer row is totally opposite. The outer canes on the left have been drawn down and under in the classical way that Bacchus usually finished off their weights, whereas the weight on the right has had the canes clipped to about half an inch in length, with no attempt at drawing the rods down. Both weights show other canes that are easily recognizable as Bacchus. The profiles and overall dimensions are practically the same.

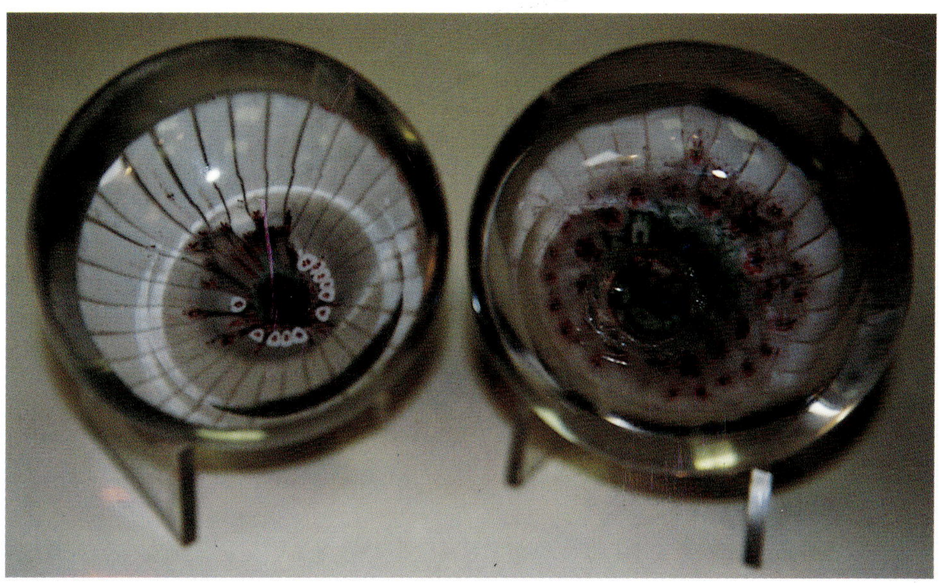

Bases of The Early Bacchus Concentrics.

The base on the right shows a very rough pontil and untidy cane ends, but that on the left shows the start of a quality finish. An attempt has been made to draw the rod ends down and under to the centre of the weight, but a few of the rods did not quite reach the centre. The pontil has been removed by grinding, with a small basal rim showing.

The makeup of the canes can be quite simple hollow tubes, but when grouped into more complex canes—which can be surrounded by a sheath of glass of any color—the canes can be compared to anything made by the foreign factories. The basic canes start as simple cogs, stars, tubes, and ruffles, with the occasional silhouette included as the central feature, or as part of a complex cane. Some of these complex canes can incorporate as many as thirty or forty other canes encased in a single rod, drawn out to make a normal sized cane. A strong magnifying glass is then required to view the content of these amazing complex canes.

The central feature cane is very often four or five times the size of the surrounding canes and is usually a simple ruffle cane enlarged to represent an open flower. Very rarely, a portrait cane of the young Queen Victoria can be found, facing left or right. These canes of the young Queen can be of various colors, including black, blue, green, white, and clear glass, and set on a contrasting, colored background. A long held belief among a few collectors and dealers was that if the head faced to dexter, then it was Bacchus, but if it faced to sinister, then it was by William Gillinder.

William T. Gillinder worked at the Bacchus glassworks for approximately four years before emigrating to America in 1854, and probably took with him a selection of canes being used by Bacchus at that time. They would have included the "Victoria Silhouette" cane that can also be found in the weights he made in America. He began work at the New England Glass Works and later started his own company called the Philadelphia Flint Glass Works, later renamed the Franklin Flint Glass Works.

Gillinder's style of paperweight making shows a similarity to many Bacchus weights, having a large central cane surrounded by pastel colored canes. His style of paperweight making would go a long way towards explaining why some weights do not conform to the Bacchus profiles given here. Several paperweights that appear in this book have Bacchus canes included, but the profiles and bases do not follow the accepted "norm" for a Bacchus weight, usually having a different base and profile. I find it hard to accept that these weights, which have been labeled "Gillinder" by many people, have all found their way back across the Atlantic from the Gillinder factory in America. I suggest that these weights were made by Gillinder and others in the early years of paperweight making at the Bacchus factory. The differences in styles and quality of some Bacchus weights would suggest the learning curves of the individual workers. Some early Bacchus weights are of an inferior nature, compared to the wonderfully skilled creations that show almost perfectly formed cane set-ups and bases in this section on Bacchus paperweights; nonetheless, are all treasured and revered pieces to the collector of this marvelous art form.

There are no dated examples of Bacchus paperweights, and no lampworked piece has ever been found.

In 1834 John Bacchus, along with several of his work colleagues, patented a small device that floated on the surface of the glass pot to help get rid of the impurities and detritus that contaminated the glass. This improved the appearance of their glass, and only rarely does one find detritus within their paperweights.

In many concentric weights by Bacchus it is possible to find an unusual squeezing of canes: the glassworker has inserted odd canes to complete the row, sometimes placing a completely unmatched cane in a row of perfectly symmetrical canes. Other examples of this oddity can be the removal of a whole, same sized cane, with two smaller ones inserted in its place. This unusual quirk appears quite frequently, and it has been said that this was a deliberate action to break up the monotony of the pattern. Or, could this be the way individual workers recognized their own work? In most cases it would have been easier to find the right cane than to put in these oddments. As paperweights were only a sideline for the company, it would be simple for the two or three workers involved in the production of weights to identify their own work with the discreet placement of a different cane or two in a perfect concentric row.

The inclusion of Mr. Bill Volkman's collection of Bacchus paperweights in this book has allowed comparisons to be made between those weights considered the best from this glasshouse and those weights which can be definitely attributed to Bacchus by the matching of canes, but have features not usually regarded as Bacchus. Illustrating these "early" and unusual weights first in the chapter may help in the identification of many more Bacchus weights that have previously gone unrecognized. Just because the weight does not conform to the well known later profiles distinguishing Bacchus weights from the other English glasshouses should not now exclude it from a Bacchus attribution. Several Bacchus weights have been added to the chapter on unknown paperweights to serve as comparisons.

Mr. Bill Volkman has been collecting English weights, and Bacchus in particular, for only eight or nine years, and now has an amazing collection of seventy Bacchus weights. Among these weights are several that are different, having most of the Bacchus features, but not all. These examples have canes which can be matched with other paperweights that have long been accepted as having the perfect profiles of a Bacchus paperweight.

It is probable that Bacchus manufactured other related items with a millefiori content, as several small toilet bottles have been attributed to this glass house.

Bacchus Early Concentric and Later Close Pack, c. 1850. ***Courtesy of Bill Volkman.***

These two paperweights show an early weight on the left and a later close packed millefiori on the right. The concentric is beginning to show the quality of canes and composition usually associated with fine Bacchus weights, having three rows of well-made ruffle canes but with an insignificant centre cane. The diameters are 3.25"; the close pack is valued at $4000 and the concentric at $1500-2000.

Profiles of Bacchus Early Concentric and Later Close Pack.

The profile of the concentric shows the differences that can be found in some of the earlier weights from this glassworks. The accepted way that Bacchus draws the outer row of tube canes towards the centre is clearly shown here. The concentric has short lengths of uneven canes, with no attempt to tidy the cane ends. This feature of leaving the cane ends uneven is very common among English paperweights.

Bases of Bacchus Early Concentric and Later Close Pack.

The difference between the two bases on these weights is quite remarkable considering that it is possible Bacchus only made paperweights for a very short time. The height of the paperweight's popularity was 1848 to around 1855, when the marketplace became saturated and production went into a steep decline. The concentric shows a broken and sharp pontil, and the close pack has a ground base with the canes gathered neatly in the centre.

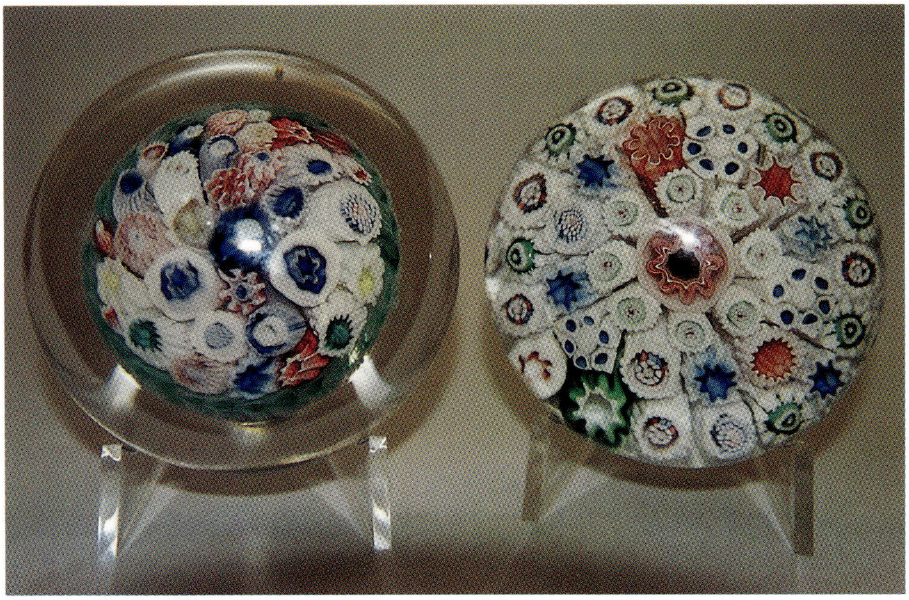

Early Bacchus Close Pack and Later Four Row Concentric, c.1850. ***Courtesy of Bill Volkman.***

The close pack on the left has a selection of large canes and a Victoria Silhouette as the central motif; several of the canes match those in the concentric and other Bacchus weights. As an early weight from Bacchus, the value is not so great as the later refined paperweights that this company produced. The close pack is valued at $750-1000, and the lovely concentric at $3000-3500.

Close-up of Early Bacchus Close Pack and Later Four Row Concentric.

The Victoria Head Silhouette cane can be seen on the left, along with a white encased, complex cane with forty-four pink, white, and blue rods, held together in a white sleeve which matches a cane in the concentric. The central feature cane of the concentric is a pink and white layered cane which is encased in clear glass and then set in a tube of white glass. These often very large centre canes in Bacchus weights can be very plain or very beautiful, as seen in this example.

Profiles of Early Close Pack and Later Four Row Concentric.

The height of the close pack is only 1.7" and the concentric is 2.1". In both weights, the outer row of tube canes has been drawn under the paperweight to the centre, with the pontil removed by grinding.

Early Close Pack, Bacchus c. 1850. Height 1.9". Dia. 3.1". $300-500. ***Courtesy of Bill Volkman.***

This may be an apprentice test piece or end-of-day weight, but a good range of canes can be seen that are recognizably Bacchus. The cane set-up has been put together rather hurriedly, and is slightly off centre and distorted.

Close Pack with Victoria Head Silhouettes, c. 1850. Height 2.4". Dia. 3.3". $600-900. ***Courtesy of Bill Volkman.***

Three silhouette canes can be seen in this close pack, which has a very pretty pastry mould central cane. Several large bubbles indicate that this was one of the earlier pieces, as does the untidy positioning of the canes. The three solid white canes also look like head canes, but have been distorted by the final encasement of glass.

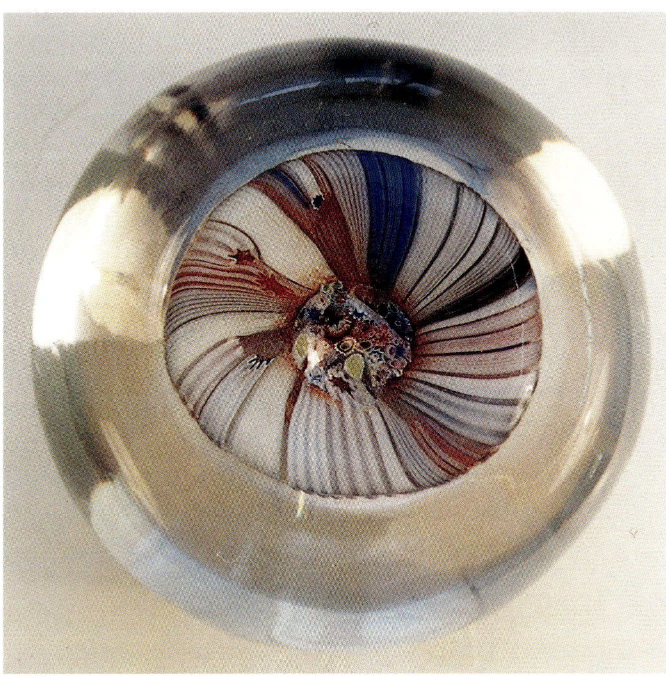

Base of Early Close Pack.

The base shows a typical Bacchus finish, with the canes on the perimeter drawn in to the centre. However, this piece shows a feature that is common on many English paperweights: a distinct ridge, which can be felt with the finger tips, where the set-up is joined to the main dome of glass. This is the first time I have seen this mark on a Bacchus weight.

Base of Close Pack with Victoria Head Silhouettes.

The outer row of canes have been drawn together to the centre of the base. The pontil has been broken off roughly and left unground. This untidy situation was corrected as the workers got better at paperweight making. It is interesting to see this progression of the glassworkers' skill, as they became proficient in one aspect, then leaving another not quite right. Bacchus must have made paperweights for several years to have progressed from these early untidy weights to their magnificent later creations.

Bacchus Concentric with Silhouettes. Height 2.3". Dia. 3.75". $4500-5000. *Courtesy of Bill Volkman.*

Twenty-six Victoria Head canes make up the centre features of this early Bacchus weight. The composition of the canes are beginning to look more acceptable, with less slippage when the final dome of glass is applied

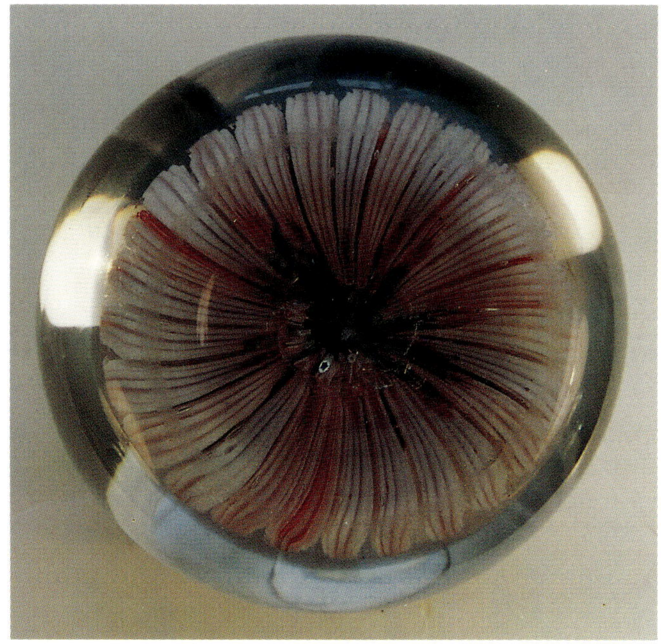

Base of Bacchus Concentric with Silhouettes.

Everything is getting better in the progress of the Bacchus paperweight production, but they have still left the pontil unground and rough and the finish to the cane ends is still untidy at this stage in the development of the paperweight.

Close-Up of Bacchus Concentric with Silhouettes.

Early Bacchus Five Row Concentric. Height 1.7". Dia. 3.5". $2000-2500. *Courtesy of Bill Volkman.*

An unusual early weight that has a top printy cut across most of the top surface. The three rows of cross canes are centred on an enlarged red and white cross, with a black centre. All the canes are neatly set with very little slippage.

Bacchus Four Row Concentric, c. 1850. Height 1.7". Dia. 3". $1000-1250. *Courtesy of Bill Volkman.*

Pale pink and blue pastel colors make this an attractive weight, but the canes have a few large bubbles in the dome which slightly spoil the overall effect of a very nice weight. The central cane cluster has a heavy white tube encasing it, which has become one of the identifying features of Bacchus paperweights.

Base of Early Bacchus Five Row Concentric.

The base is almost perfectly formed, except for the rough pontil. The cane ends are finished to a neat circle, allowing a mirror image of the crown to be viewed through the base of the weight.

Base of Bacchus Four Row Concentric.

The last remnants of the unground pontil can just be seen. The pontil mark is in a slight concavity and does not interfere with the base sitting flat on the surface. Only when the pontil rod was broken off and protruding did they grind it off. A small porthole is left in the centre to allow a view inside the weight.

Bacchus Close Packed Millefiori, c. 1850. Dia 3.6". $4000-5000.
Author's Collection.

This is a superb example of a close pack and contains 140 canes, most of them complex, using almost all of the colors in the Bacchus repertoire. The complex combination canes are made by bunching the basic cane rods and encasing them in either colored or clear glass. Several of the larger canes are combinations of complex canes, themselves being held together and encased in an outer layer of glass. The cane combinations are infinite, the only limitation being the glassworkers imagination. The seemingly hollow tubes are in fact filled with clear glass and encased within a sleeve of usually white, blue, or green glass, which seem to be the predominant colors used by Bacchus. The canes are set in an apparently haphazard way, but the whole effect is pleasing to the eye, the observer being led all over the surface by the occasional placing of a cane with a stronger color. This weight also has an oak leaf cane; the pale green serrated edges are encased by a tube of white glass.

Profile of Close Packed Millefiori. Height 2.25".

This side view reveals how the outside row of interspersed colored canes has been pulled down and under to achieve a basket effect. This hides any untidy cane ends which may have been seen by looking beneath the weight. The canes used for the outer row are all tubes in soft pastel green and blue, with the occasional use of a stronger color to give the appearance of a spoke effect.

Base of Close Packed Millefiori.

The base shows a typical Bacchus finish, with the rods drawn down and under to the centre of the weight. The pontil is broken off and the base is lightly hollow ground to remove all traces. This very often leaves a small window through which a mirror image of the top surface can be observed. The basal ring can be as wide as 0.5" in many weights, and having been pushed around for nearly 150 years can show considerable wear.

Bacchus Five row Concentric, c. 1850. Dia. 3.5". $3500-4000. Author's Collection.

This concentric weight has an outer row of hollow green tubes set next to large white ruffles. Amongst these white ruffles you will find a "rogue" cane as described in the introduction to this chapter on Bacchus. This odd cane is the same as the central large white ruffle. I have never seen a Bacchus weight with more than one "rogue," but they are quite common and sometimes easily spotted. I am convinced this was a recognition cane used by a particular worker at the Bacchus factory to recognize his own work. Also note the two small canes deliberately squeezed into the row of red and white canes near the centre; surely it would have been easier to have shuffled the canes around and inserted a matching sized cane instead of these two oddballs. It has been suggested by Paul Hollister in the *Encyclopaedia of Paperweights* that this was a deliberate act, possibly designed to break the monotony of the pattern. This may be the case, but I prefer my signature cane theory.

Profile of Five row Concentric. Height 2.6".

The cushion of canes rises just over half way into the dome. The outer row of hollow cogged tubes are drawn down and under to form the basket and finish the base neatly.

Base of Five row Concentric.

The view from beneath shows the spoke wheel effect achieved by the placement of slightly darker canes when the outer circle was being set up. I am sure the workers were indeed trying to improve the base, and must have understood the effect these darker canes have on the appearance of the base. The canes are drawn right into the centre, but a view of the inside of the weight is still possible through the "porthole."

Bacchus Victoria Head Four Row Concentric, c. 1850. Dia. 3.5". $3500-4000. *Author's Collection.*

This example shows a silhouette of the young Queen Victoria. The central white profile sits on a royal blue background surrounded by a row of open white ruffle canes that are slightly translucent and flared like a half open Convolvolus. The next row of pink and white canes can be seen through the white ruffle canes, highlighting the delicate nature of the cane coloring. The solid, clear glass centres of the ruffle cannot be seen, and this is a truly remarkable cane. The canes are pulled down into the centre of the weight, as with a bouquet of flowers. Although of apparent simple construction, this ruffle cane is used to great effect in this lovely Bacchus example. Note that once more a "rogue" cane appears in the next row of dark green open cog canes, totally different from its neighbours, but placed there so the worker could say "I made that, that's one of mine."

Profile of Victoria Head Concentric. Height 2.3".

Again we have the typical Bacchus profile, the sides emerging from beneath the base to rise smoothly up and over, forming the cushion outline. The canes rise well into the dome to completely fill the weight when viewed from above. A few small air bubbles are trapped inside this piece, but do not detract from its beauty.

Base of Victoria Head Concentric.

The canes are drawn down and under to the very centre, leaving a small porthole opening of less than a quarter of an inch, but all of the canes can still be seen in microcosm, in perfect form, even the Victoria Silhouette, which is down to the size of a pin head. The outer ring of canes forms a basket with the centre of the weight very lightly hollow ground, to remove all traces of the pontil mark. The wide basal ring reaches right out to the side of the weight.

Bacchus Four Row Concentric, c. 1850. Dia. 3.5". $4500-5500.
Author's Collection.

This is an extremely fine example of the glassmaker's art, in near perfect condition with only one small piece of detritus floating in the crown of the weight. The four rows of canes surround an amazing example of a complex cane. The central cane contains twenty-three miniature canes which, if full size, would themselves make a fine paperweight. The next row is made up of ruffle cane bound together with a layer of white and then encased in a layer of royal blue. The exceedingly complex cane has been described as a "shield cane," as it looks like an ancient Greek soldier's shield. The outer three rows, although well constructed and quite beautiful in their own right, cannot match these central beauties. The overall effect of the royal blue against the pastel pinks and whites, striking but not clashing with its neighbours, shows what true artists the glassworkers at Bacchus were. In this weight there are no "rogue" canes; to have included one would surely have been of no credit to the artist at all and would have been an act of defilement in a weight of such outstanding beauty. I am sure the glassworker must have thought the same. However, as I examined the base before putting pen to paper, I was astonished to see that "rogue" cane in miniature. On close examination with a magnifying glass, it is possible to see a darker colored cane lurking on the inside of the perfectly formed porthole. This surely proves that whoever made this weight wants us to recognize his artistry, and let us know he is there. This "rogue" cane links us back to the 1850s and a Bacchus worker with a wry smile and a twinkle in his eye. "Find me if you can," he must have thought. Well, we have, and we know you are there!

Profile of Four Row Concentric.

The profile has the classic Bacchus shape. The sides start well under the base and rise swiftly and smoothly to form a low domed top. The outer row of blue, white, and yellow canes are drawn down and under to the centre of the base.

Base of Four Row Concentric.

The base is almost as beautiful as the top; the crown of canes radiating out from the central porthole are set very precisely. The central porthole allows one to see into the interior of the weight to view it in miniature. Even the porthole has been finished off to a startlingly precise circle. The pontil has been removed by grinding a slight concavity and leaving a basal ring of 0.3".

Bacchus Spaced Concentric with Victoria Head, c. 1850. Dia. 3.125". $1750-2500. *Author's Collection.*

This is a very interesting weight which has been the subject of much discussion as to its attribution. At first glance, some experts have said "Gillinder" because the profile does not conform to the low domed cushion as seen in previous Bacchus examples. Secondly, the Victoria Head cane goes all the way through the weight and exits the base leaving a small protrusion. The base is left as the paperweight left the pontil rod, unground with the weight pivoting on the pontil mark. The diameter is only 3.125". against the normal 3.25" to 3.5". and the height is 2.25". The silhouette cane is similar to the recognized Bacchus heads, with a good comparison on page 151 of Sibylle Jargstorf's book *Paperweights*. The weight illustrated in *Paperweights* also shows identical composite canes to those seen in the three rows of spaced concentric canes in this weight. The protruding cane in the base is also not quite unique, as a concentric Bacchus paperweight with a torsade handle (which can be seen on a following page) also has a cane that reaches all the way through to the base. The ability to match the two types of canes used in this weight with other Bacchus pieces leaves me in no doubt that it would be reasonable to make the Bacchus attribution. I would suggest that this weight could have been made by Gillinder during his time at Bacchus. The complex canes are of a quite delicate construction, being two rows of very small solid rods and cog canes, gathered together and encased in a white pastry mould cane. The three rows are then set into a very dark blue ground. The middle row of canes is not a circle, but has five sides. This paperweight was bought at a Birmingham auction house, several years ago, and was catalogued as nineteenth century Bacchus.

Profile of Spaced Concentric. Height 2.25".

The profile of this weight has the same smooth, curving sides, rising from beneath the base to a slightly domed top. The outside row of canes are 0.5" long and look to be pushed into the dark blue colored ground. Bacchus made several weights with the "sodden snow" ground which is almost identical to the French "Clichy" version. The colored ground cushion rises just over half way into the dome.

Base of Spaced Concentric.

The base is similar to the recognized Bacchus shape, except for the protruding cane. If the pontil had been ground to leave it slightly concave, the base would conform to the accepted shape.

Bacchus Concentric Bouquet with Torsade Handle, c. 1850. Height 2.125". Dia. 3.75". $2500-3000. *Courtesy of Marleen Van Horne White.*

This splendid Bacchus weight has several unusual features. If you look closely you will see that four of the five rows of canes are different variations of crosses. This weight is an important reference piece because of these different crosses. I have been unable, in the time available, to research this weight to match the crosses with other Bacchus pieces. The five rows of pink, white, and very pale blue canes are centred on a large red and white cog cane, with a black core. This central cane is drawn all the way through the weight to reach the base. The pontil has been broken off to leave a small indentation. It has not been ground as with the majority of Bacchus weights, and the base is similar to the preceding Victoria Head spaced concentric. The bouquet is completely encircled by a red, white, and pale blue torsade to form the handle of a basket. This handle lies just beneath the surface of the glass dome.

Bacchus Five Row Concentric, c. 1850. Dia 3.5". $2500-3000. *Courtesy of Anne Anderson.*

Although this weight is very desirable and a welcome addition to anyone's collection, it is not of the highest Bacchus standard. It could have been an excellent piece but for the rather sloppy placement of the canes. It would appear that the canes have slipped when the set-up had the dome of glass added in the picking-up process. The five rows of canes are centred on a large red cog cane, encased in white. This type of large cane is the central feature in many Bacchus weights; it is usually of a simple construction, but always three or four times the size of normal canes, giving the paperweight a focal point. The yellow canes at the outside edge are unusual, in that glassmakers tended to avoid the color yellow. This was because of problems with the color burning to a brown if overheated in the furnace. The profile and base exactly match the Bacchus style, with the outside row being drawn down and under the base, leaving a small porthole to view the inside. The base is lightly ground to remove the pontil mark.

Base of Concentric Bouquet with Torsade Handle.

The profile is quite low in proportion to the diameter, and the bouquet would have been enhanced if a little more glass had been added to the dome to increase the magnifying properties of the glass. The bouquet rises almost to the top of the dome and is covered by very little glass.

Bacchus Close Packed with Silhouette cane, c, 1850. $2500-3000. Dia 3.5". *Courtesy of Anne Anderson.*

A tightly packed paperweight with predominantly small canes. There are larger canes, but of a simple composition. The surface is a riot of color—blues, reds, pale greens, and whites all radiating outwards from the central large cog cane. The canes are much smaller than many Bacchus examples but the mixture of small and large canes are quite compatible in this very nice illustration of a close pack. Note the blue on white petal type canes; could this be an early attempt at a flower? It may be that some of the weights with these small, simply constructed canes and complex canes were early attempts at paperweight making. The factory, probably having seen Baccarat examples appearing in the stationer's shops around 1845-50, began to copy these very popular items. In this weight you can also see the Victoria Head Silhouette cane. This example has a white background with a black head, set amongst the canes near the edge of the weight. The head has a long neck, similar to the spaced concentric on earlier pages.

Profile of Close Packed with Silhouette. Height 2.5".

The profile shows a low cushion with the canes rising well into the dome. The side canes are drawn down and under to the centre of the base, leaving a small porthole. The base is slightly hollow ground to remove the pontil, and leaves a quite wide basal ring of 0.25". The colors of the canes drawn into the centre show that no attempt was made to create a spoke effect, as can be seen on some weights from Bacchus, which makes me convinced that this was an early weight from the Bacchus Glassworks.

Bacchus Five Row Concentric, c. 1850. $3750-4500. Height 2.3". Dia 3.6". ***Courtesy of Anne Anderson.***

This is a superb example from Bacchus with an extraordinary central cane of magnum proportions. The whole weight is of a very precise structure with pastel shades that blend into one another in a subtle and contrived way. The canes are all complex and very precisely set with the exception of one "rogue" cane; notice the white cane set squarely in the row of salmon pink canes. The central "magnum" cane is made up of layer upon layer of ice cream white glass. The initial white moulded cane must have been dipped into the white glass four or five times to achieve this effect. The complex ruffle canes in the outer row are encased in the thinnest layer of pale blue and are then surrounded by the precisely set deep blue tube canes; these are then drawn beneath the weight to leave everything nice and tidy. As it is possible that only three to four hundred weights were made by Bacchus, it is probable that the weights made with the "rogue" canes were made by the same man. He was a man of meticulous artistry, and his weights stand out from the others.

Bacchus Close Packed Millefiori, c. 1850. Height 2.5". Dia 3.6". $4750. ***Courtesy of The Stone Gallery, Burford, England.***

Tightly packed canes in soft pastel shades make this weight very desirable. Pinks, pale greens, blues, and yellows are the predominant colors of the simple and complex canes, all shuffled together in a random mixture. The outer row of green and white tube canes are drawn down and under the weight to the centre to form the stave basket that is common on all the quality concentric and close packed Bacchus weights. Several of the "Greek shield" canes appear randomly along with mainly ruffle and cog canes, all tidily placed around the large central feature cane. This unusual large central cane has two thick coats of blue and white, which encase a very fine and delicate centre; these heavy coats of glass rather detract from the delicate nature of the whole weight. However, this paperweight is in fine condition and contains enough variety to keep the collector in paperweight "heaven."

Bacchus/Gillinder Six row Concentric with Victoria Head, c. 1850. Dia. 2.9". $2000-2250. *Courtesy of Anne Anderson.*

This paperweight has been attributed to William T. Gillinder, a fine paperweight maker, who worked at the Bacchus factory for several years before emigrating to the USA in 1854. However, on close examination the construction and set-up of the canes around the silhouette cane suggest that it may be by Gillinder but possibly that it was made during his time at the Bacchus works. The soft coloring suggests that it is of English manufacture, and the general coloring of the canes, the simple hollow tubes, and the ruffle canes all seem to point towards Bacchus. The Victoria Head looks the same as others already shown in this book, and is the same as the Victoria Silhouette Heads that appear in recognized Gillinder weights produced in America which he probably took with him on leaving Bacchus. The weight was bought in England, and has no history of previous owners. Unfortunately, without factory records or designs it comes down to personal opinion and conjecture as to the attribution of this weight. Whoever made this paperweight, Gillinder or another Bacchus worker, can be proud to have produced this superbly made piece, as I know the present owner is proud to own such a treasure.

Base of Bacchus/Gillinder.

The base is also very similar to Bacchus, with the outside row of hollow tube canes drawn down and under to the centre of the weight, leaving a small porthole through which the weight can be viewed internally, and is exactly the same way Bacchus finished off their weights. The base is also slightly hollow ground to remove all traces of the pontil mark.

Profile of Bacchus/Gillinder. Height 1.9".

The cushion profile also suggests Bacchus. The canes rise well into the roof of the weight as do many Bacchus cushion set-ups. The size is only slightly smaller than the better known of the Bacchus weights, but if it was indeed made by Gillinder, then this would be of a similar size to his known paperweights produced in America.

Baccus Close Packed with Central Victoria Head, c. 1850. Dia. 3.125". *Courtesy of Hulbert of Dudley Collection, Broadfield House Museum, Kingswinford, England.*

The rather crudely made canes suggest that this was an early weight from the Bacchus factory. Although there are several very complex canes in this weight, they are constructed using simple rod bundles. The most striking cane is the silhouette of a "Young Head." This cane of the young Queen Victoria would be of her around 1850. Of all the silhouette canes of the Queen I have seen, I have never seen a cane which shows the Queen in latter years. This suggests that these weights with a head were all made around the peak "Classic" period of production. This "Classic" period is thought to be from 1845 to 1852. During this time dated paperweights by Baccarat and Saint Louis are known. In addition to the central silhouette, there are three other heads buried deep inside the complex canes. These miniature silhouettes have been reduced to the size of a pinhead, but are perfect in every detail. The canes show a wide variety of colors including strong yellows and blues. Several white on red crosses appear to the right hand side of the weight. The large complex canes are constructed of random colored canes with no attempt at a pattern.

Base.

The profile of this weight conforms to the recognized shape and style of Bacchus, the low cushion falling steeply to finish under the weight and leaving a small porthole. The outer row of canes are used to hide the untidy cane ends very effectively, all drawn to the centre to form a basket. The pontil mark can still be seen, and has not been ground away. The pontil has been snapped off sufficiently close to the base, leaving a slight indentation to save the grinding process. The basal ring is nearly half an inch wide. The size is 3.125" diameter and 1.80" high. Could this weight be another early Gillinder? The rough pontil and slightly smaller size may be clues to the attribution. The paperweight was donated to the Broadfield House Glass Museum, Kingswinford, England by a local family. Broadfield House is only ten miles from Birmingham city centre, where Bacchus and Islington Glassworks were located in the 1850s.

Bacchus Five Row Concentric, c. 1850. Height 2.3". Dia 3.5". $4500-5000. *Courtesy of Colin McCallien.*

A truly beautiful paperweight from Bacchus, the central white and mauve cane has the delicate nature of fine lace. The components of this central cane are so thin as to be almost translucent. My attempt to photograph the centre does not do it justice. The rest of the rows are also of a standard that cannot be bettered for composition, coloring, and complexity, even by the best of Saint Louis and Baccarat. The canes are very tightly packed together, with hardly room to push in a needle. The pastel shades blend together in a most delightful way. But once again, lurking in the outer row of blue canes is the "rogue." Every other cane in that row has a centre of a red ruffle, except for one that has a white ruffle. This can be seen on the right hand side of the paperweight. The weight is in fine condition without bruises and scratches. Beautiful objects, appreciated by discerning buyers and collectors, can remain in pristine condition for many, many years, carefully handed down through generations of a family. The outer row of canes are drawn down and under to the centre, and lightly ground to remove all traces of the pontil mark. The profile is that of a low cushion.

Bacchus Four Row Concentric, c. 1850. Height 2.3". Dia 3.5". $3250-3750. *Courtesy of Colin McCallien.*

This is another superb weight in terms of construction and subtle coloring. The best of the Bacchus complex canes are in a league of their own, mainly comprising ruffle and cog canes and usually encased in a colored glass, but occasionally in clear glass. The combination of pink and blue pastels was a favourite of the Bacchus designers, and distinguishes the weights made by this glasshouse from other English and French paperweight makers. In this weight, I cannot find a "rogue" cane, but I did not look beneath the piece for a sometimes tiny cane, drawn down to the base and now and again seen on the edge of the porthole. The central cane looks somewhat crude and clumsy after the lovely central cane in the previous piece. Although a very striking cane, the central part does not look finished, the inner white cog has not been joined together. This spoils what could have been a special weight from Bacchus.

Bacchus Miniature Close Pack with Victoria Silhouette, c. 1850. Dia 1.7". $1200-1500. *Courtesy of Colin McCallien.*

This is a rare Bacchus miniature containing one large and four small Victoria Heads. The four small heads are hidden in the centres of a red and white cog cane, directly above the central cane, with two more at 2 o'clock and 7 o'clock and another even smaller directly in front of the central head cane. The heads are all dark blue on white and look as though they are all from the same cane rod. The incredibly small size to which the canes can be drawn, without losing any detail, means that many of these heads go unseen, only to be spotted at some later date, much to the delight of the owner. Close packs have a habit of turning up unknown canes, as with the recently identified oak leaves found in some Bacchus weights and illustrated in *The Glass Menagerie* by John Hawley. Many of the seemingly hollow canes are in fact filled with clear or colored glass, with the majority of canes being cogs and ruffles. Although only a miniature, the profile is exactly the same as a full size weight. The outer row of blue and white tube canes are pulled down and under to make a basket.

Base of Miniature. Height 1.3".

The base shows the typical Bacchus finish, but in this case the pontil has been left unground. The pontil rod has been snapped off close to the base, to leave a small indentation and save the grinding procedure.

Bacchus Five Row Concentric, c. 1850. Dia. 3.5". $2500-3000. *Courtesy of Colin McCallien.*

The central pastry mould cane is made by repeatedly dipping into clear and white glass, building up the layers to form a flower-like cane. Even an all white cane çan be used to great effect in the centre of a weight. The dark blue canes surrounding the centre highlight and draws attention to the flower. The third row of pale blue canes are simple cane rods of various colors surrounded by a row of darker blue rods, and then encased in a thin layer of clear glass. Viewed under a strong magnifying glass, this cane looks like a complete paperweight in miniature. This could have been an extremely good weight but is let down by a little untidiness in the selection of cane sizes around the central featured cane. The two outside rows are neatly packed in place but the next two rows could have been arranged with a bit more care. For this reason, although I looked, I did not really expect to find a "rogue" cane, which seems to identify only the better and precisely made pieces, but this would still be a welcome addition to anyone's collection.

Bacchus Five Row Concentric, c. 1850. Dia. 3.4". $3250-3750.
Courtesy of Colin McCallien.

A well constructed paperweight filled with complexly made ruffle canes. The dark blue and pink shield canes are a welcome addition in any Bacchus paperweight. This rather striking cane frames the pale colors of the next two rows beautifully. The row of white canes are mixed ruffles, in no apparent pattern, but the next row of egg shell blue and pink complex canes clash with the harsh yellow color of the cog canes framing the central feature cane. The large red and white encased pastry mould is skillfully made, and canes of this quality deservedly sit as the main feature in this lovely paperweight.

Bacchus Five Row Concentric, c. 1850. Dia 3.5". $2500-3000.
Courtesy of Colin McCallien.

This paperweight is made using only simple canes in comparison to some of the extremely complex examples we have seen in previous weights. This does not detract from the quality of the weight in itself, but what does spoil what could have been a superb weight is the use of the small rods to pack out the central feature cane, presumably to stop the canes moving before being encased with the finishing dome of glass. By the insertion of these small odd canes, the glassworker who made the set-up has in fact distorted the row surrounding the central cane. Why colored rods were used, when clear glass was the obvious answer, I cannot understand. The whole paperweight is still a "Bacchus" and very desirable to all but the most fastidious of collectors. The weight conforms to the Bacchus style, the outer row is drawn down and into the centre of the base, to form a small porthole. The pontil has been removed by hollow grinding.

Bacchus Close Packed Millefiori, c. 1850. Dia. 2.9". $4000-4500. ***Collection of Karen & Paul Dunlop, Photo © 1997 Papier Presse.***

This is a lovely example of a Bacchus close pack, using mainly blue, pink, and soft mint green canes. The complex canes are formed by bundling together ten or more simple canes, and then encased in a thin layer of clear glass to bind them together. Many Bacchus large complex canes are encased in a layer of colored glass, but in this beautiful piece no colored encasing has been used, leaving the colors to contrast sharply with their neighbour. The mint green canes are always a pleasure to see in a Bacchus weight; the pastel shade adds a softness to the otherwise bold colors in this paperweight.

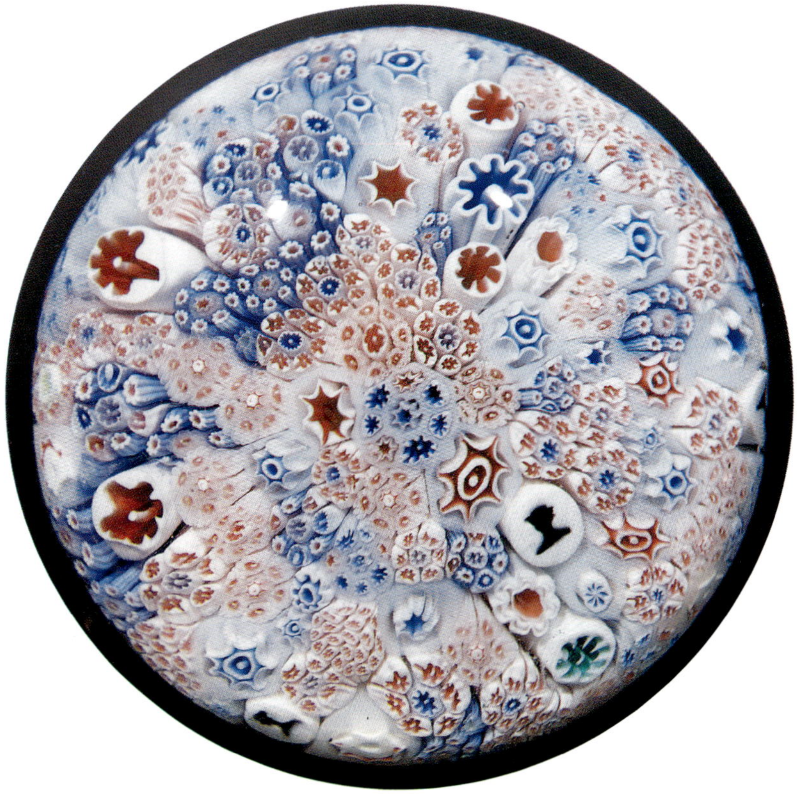

Bacchus Close Packed Millefiori, with Three Victoria Heads, c. 1850. Dia. 3.5".$4500-5000. ***Collection of Karen & Paul Dunlop, Photo © 1997 Papier Presse.***

A close pack similar to the previous paperweight using predominantly pink and blue complex canes. However, this weight has the added advantage of three Victoria Heads, which adds to the value of the piece. The weight has pink and white complex canes almost identical to the previous weight, with the blue canes being softer in color than the former piece. The surface of pinks and blues is broken up by the insertion of stronger deep pink canes encased in a sheath of white glass. Victoria Heads were a feature of many Bacchus weights, and can sometimes be found as the centres of complex canes. There is another unusual cane at the bottom edge of this photograph, a pale green, serrated edged cane that looks similar to an oak leaf. I always look for the "rogue" cane when first seeing a new weight, and the last place I would expect to find one is in a close pack, but this green cane stands out in the predominantly pink, white and blues for all to see.

Bacchus Spaced Millefiori in "Sodden Snow," c. 1850. Dia. 3.25". $4000-4500. ***Collection of Karen & Paul Dunlop, Photo © 1997 Papier Presse.***

One of the rarest of Bacchus paperweights. The "sodden snow" is a ground of slightly off white glass into which the canes are set flush. The canes in this weight vary tremendously, but are not the most beautiful from the Bacchus variety of complex canes. The cane that is certainly the most unusual is the red complex cane set in a block of clear glass with a red lining. This "square" cane is a most exceptional find in any English or French paperweight. The cane must have been flattened on the marver plate after being drawn out while still soft and pliable. The placement of the small odd canes next to the large complex ones makes me wonder what the glassworkers were trying to achieve, as the large complex canes would have been quite sufficient to complete the paperweight to a very high standard, without the inclusion of these odd bits of cane. The paperweight is attractive and very desirable to Bacchus collectors.

Bacchus Close Pack, in "Autumn" Colors, c. 1850. Dia. 3.25". $4500-5000. ***Collection of Karen & Paul Dunlop, Photo © 1997 Papier Presse.***

The colors described by the owners of this weight as "Autumn" are appropriate, as the cream and russet colors remind me of autumn Chrysanthemums. The reds are almost brown, and an unusual color to see in a Bacchus paperweight. The occasional pastel green and blue canes are spaced across the surface for added effect. Without the insertion of the blue canes this weight would have been a superb carpet ground using the russet and cream canes alone. It is still a very desirable paperweight as it stands, and would be hotly contested at auction.

Bacchus Five Row Concentric, c. 1850. Dia 3.5". $4500-5000. ***Collection of Karen & Paul Dunlop, Photo © 1997 Papier Presse.***

A precisely constructed concentric of the highest workmanship. The Bacchus concentric paperweight was a match for, or even superior to, many paperweights from France or Bohemia. The pastel shading of the colors blends with, and does not clash with its neighbour in this lovely example. The outer row of tube canes are pulled down and under to make the "stave basket" used by this glasshouse to such great effect. Most Bacchus paperweights have this "basket" which finishes off the base of the weight so tidily. It is probable that the workers at Bacchus were greatly influenced by the French glasshouses of Clichy, Saint Louis, and Baccarat, who were making exceptional paperweights from 1845. Many French glassworkers are known to have migrated to the Birmingham area during this period of rapid expansion following the removal of the glass tax. Bacchus did not just copy the French makers, they added extra input to the making and coloring of the complex canes. The use of pastel colors places Bacchus apart from the rest of the paperweights producers at that time. The combination of the blue and pink segments in the complex cane in the third row from the centre is a particularly beautiful cane. The central feature cane is strikingly simple to look at, but would have taken skill and thought to make.

Bacchus White Four Row Concentric, c. 1850. Dia. 3.4". $5000-6000. ***Collection of Karen & Paul Dunlop, Photo © 1997 Papier Presse.***

This wonderful paperweight in almost pure white is an example of the thought that goes into the best of the Bacchus paperweights. The rows of white ruffle canes would have made a striking weight on their own, but the inclusion of the faintest hint of ice blue, in one row, makes the weight outstanding. The worker who made this weight must have seen the effect sunlight has on deep snow drifts. When sunlight passes through ice crystals, a blue fluorescence can be seen deep inside a snowdrift or iceberg. The central pastry mould cane is set in a bowl of clear glass, and does nothing to detract from the simplistic beauty of this special paperweight from the masters of the paperweight artform. I have not seen beneath this weight but would not be surprised to see some kind of identity mark in the shape of an odd cane, to say "I made this, that signature mark is mine."

Bacchus Four Row Concentric, c. 1850. Dia 3.5". $3500-4000. ***Collection of Karen & Paul Dunlop, Photo © 1997 Papier Presse.***

Another fine concentric with the little used yellow canes surrounding the central, featured cane. The tried and tested combination of pinks and blues are used to great effect in this very precisely made paperweight. Cogs and ruffles make up the delicate, lacy complex canes, with as many as twenty or more canes used to make up the pink and white complex canes in the third row. The central feature cane is encased in a thick layer of white which surrounds the different layers of deep red and white cogs and scallops.

Bacchus Five Row Concentric Millefiori, c. 1850. Dia 3.3". $3500-4000. ***Collection of Karen & Paul Dunlop, Photo © 1997 Papier Presse.***

The central feature cane stands out, well surrounded by a layer of deep blue glass. The central cog cane is simply made, but with the use of the dark blue, it has an eye catching quality to it. The Canary yellow and white tube canes are a welcome addition in this paperweight. The row on the outside of the yellow canes are filled with all sorts of colored rods and tubes, including greens, yellow and blues.

Bacchus Five Row Concentric, c. 1850. Dia. 3". $3000-3500. ***Collection of Karen & Paul Dunlop, Photo © 1997 Papier Presse.***

This fine concentric has a row of complex canes encased in the rarely seen olive color. The predominantly colored pink and white rows are separated by the olive canes. The rows are centred around the very simple, large red and white cog cane. Bacchus had a way of leaning the canes outwards to form a "bouquet of flowers" effect. This was achieved by encasing the tapered canes with a varying thickness of clear glass, giving the appearance of separation between the individual canes.

Bacchus Four Row Concentric Millefiori, c. 1850. Dia. 3.5". $5000-6000. ***Collection of Karen & Paul Dunlop, Photo © 1997 Papier Presse.***

The much stronger coloring of this paperweight makes it a little unusual from most of the softer colored Bacchus pieces. The pink and blue complex shield canes in the centre contrast sharply with the almost black, dark green canes next to them. This weight was perhaps a test piece to see the effect of pastel and darker colors together. This is a paperweight of superior quality and precision, and has the "rogue" cane in the row between the green and the blue and white rows. The outer row is pulled down and under to make the stave basket. The outer row, used to form the basket, is nearly always a hollow tube cane. The cane seems solid but is a colored lining with clear glass filling the centre. The clear glass was cheaper and more plentiful than the blue glass, and achieved the same appearance when finished.

Bacchus Close Packed with Victoria Heads, c. 1850. Dia. 3.3". $3000-3500. ***Collection of Karen & Paul Dunlop, Photo © 1997 Papier Presse.***

There is plenty of interest in this paperweight, with its variety of colors and canes. Most canes are pastel shades with the exception of a few deep blue and ruby colors. But the outstanding features are the Victoria Heads, all five of them. Notice how the heads are looking left and right; this all depends on the way the person who sets the canes in the ring, prior to being picked up by the glassmaker, handles the individual cane. He could set the cane up or down to face either direction, as he chose. Also appearing in this weight are the "oak" leaf canes, some singly and as part of a complex cane. These "oak" leaves are a welcome addition in Bacchus weights, as many have gone unnoticed in the past.

Bacchus Close Packed with Victoria Heads, c. 1850. Dia. 3.4". $3000-3500. ***Collection of Karen & Paul Dunlop, Photo © 1997 Papier Presse.***

This almost identical close pack has the same cane combinations as the previous weight, and was almost certainly made by the same glassworker on the same day. In this weight there are only two "heads" showing, but many "oak" leaves.

Bacchus Encased Overlay, c. 1850. Dia. 2.9". $6000-7000. ***Collection of Karen & Paul Dunlop, Photo © 1997 Papier Presse.***

This is one of the rarest of Bacchus paperweights. The tuft of canes are sealed into clear glass, and then dipped or rolled into white glass to overlay the weight; the weight was then returned to another furnace for a further coating of dark blue glass. At this stage the weight is cooled and annealed. The cold weight then had a printy or facet window ground on the top to allow the inner design to be seen. Now visible are the two layers of blue and white glass. The tricky part was to encase the paperweight in a thick layer of clear glass. It is at this point that the glassworkers had many problems, and the reason why "encased" paperweights are so rare and such an achievement for the glassmaker. In trying to reheat the paperweight to the stage where it is again soft and pliable, the temperature has to be increased very slowly; if heated too quickly the weight will form stress cracks. Due to the many weights lost and scrapped at this stage, the glassworkers deemed it unviable and this explains the rarity of this type of paperweight. Modern paperweight makers have told me that a cold paperweight would need to be reheated in a computer controlled furnace, very slowly over forty-eight hours, to achieve any success with this encasing process. The Scottish paperweight maker John Deacons has been making encased weights recently, and seems to be having considerable success with this method. Bacchus tried many variations of paperweight types, and it would seem they had the skilled workers who could produce anything required. The paperweight motif design in itself is not of the highest standard from the Bacchus factory; the canes are complex and formed into a "bouquet" which has allowed too much clear glass to be seen. If the glassworkers were experiencing lots of problems with this encasing process then it makes sense to use a simply made set-up of canes to experiment with. Although not the most beautiful, it is certainly one of the prized pieces in this collection because of its rarity.

Bacchus Mushroom with Torsade, c. 1850. Dia. 3.6". $6500-7500. ***Collection of Karen & Paul Dunlop, Photo © 1997 Papier Presse.***

The use of a spiral torsade always makes the weight look special, and this weight is no exception—beautifully constructed and lovely to look at. The central feature cane has been made by combining seven ruffle canes around a pink floret, giving it a delicate lacy look. The canes radiate outwards to the pink lined hollow tubes which are then pulled downwards to make the thin stem of the mushroom. The blue and white spiral torsade ties the whole thing together, like a "bridesmaid's" posy of flowers.

Bacchus Paneled Carpet Ground, c. 1850. Dia. 3.25". $6000-7000. ***Collection of Karen & Paul Dunlop, Photo © 1997 Papier Presse.***

This is a paperweight with a composed preciseness that is a feature of the best of the paperweights from Bacchus, but a second look shows how they also distorted the pattern in so many of their weights. We shall never know for sure the reasons why, but if you count the colored groups of canes that set the style of the weight, you will see three blue sets and three pink sets, and then we have an odd set of red canes, either just pushed in to fill out the space or a "rogue" set. The paperweight is indeed a delight to view, the central cluster of canes are all complex bundles of simple rods and tubes, and when conjoined they make attractive canes. The outside row of canes show a hint of lilac, and when pulled beneath the weight to finish off, makes a lovely stave basket.

Bacchus Carpet Ground, c. 1850. Dia. 3.25". $3000-3500. ***Collection of Karen & Paul Dunlop, Photo © 1997 Papier Presse.***

The white canes in this carpet ground are all made up of ruffle canes. Each one is encased in a tube of white glass, giving a light and airy appearance to the whole weight; with the inclusion of the lightly colored spaced canes, just enough color is added to make the weight special. Several of the canes are of the palest lilac possible. Bacchus made colored canes so light in appearance as to be almost translucent. The merest hint of color was enough to break up the stark white canes.

Bacchus Close Pack, c. 1850. Dia. 3.3". $4500-5500. ***Collection of Karen & Paul Dunlop, Photo © 1997 Papier Presse.***

The close pack was a popular paperweight with all the French and English glassworks. It was a good way of disposing of all the odd canes at the end of the day, and the weight was very popular with the buying public. The canes were never set out in any particular way, as the random spacing gave the best effect. I never get tired of looking at these pieces, even after seeing a weight many, many times; I am always hopeful I may spot something I missed earlier. The canes in this piece show a good selection of colors and styles. The weight is nicely composed and tightly packed together. The colors are strong in this weight, with the yellows and blues standing out. The central ruffle cane, although simply made, is an attractive feature of this paperweight.

Bacchus Close Pack, c. 1850. Dia 3.3". $3000-3500. ***Collection of Karen & Paul Dunlop, Photo © 1997 Papier Presse.***

A close pack with very similar canes as the previous example but this one has the white canes described as "sodden snow." The canes are off white with a pure white centre. It is an unusual cane to find in a close pack, but the canes must have been left from a production run on "sodden snow" weights. The large dark blue cog cane is also not seen very often in Bacchus weights; although it looks like a simple cane it was a difficult cane to construct. The weight has an outside row of white canes to form the stave basket. This finishes the paperweight off very cleanly indeed.

Bacchus Spaced Concentric, c. 1850. Dia. 3.2". $2500-3000. ***Collection of Karen & Paul Dunlop, Photo © 1997 Papier Presse.***

This spaced concentric is set out very precisely; the canes are all set around the central pastry mould in a white sleeve. This central pastry mould has a core of ruby glass which has been dipped eight times to give it the layered look. This type of cane can be found in many canes from the French maker "Clichy." It is probable that migrant workers from France took part in paperweight making throughout the English glass industry, and perhaps they helped at the Bacchus glassworks. Most of the canes in this weight are of the open type; the open canes look hollow but are filled with clear glass. The open canes are pulled down at the base to make a cornet shape and are a Bacchus specialty. The canes in the central row also are special; the white cog surrounds a blue layer of glass which has seven stardust canes inside. Also seen in this weight are several complex canes on the outside edge which have as centres the head of Victoria in miniature, drawn out to the size of a pin head.

Bacchus Faceted Overlay, c. 1850. Dia. 3.5". $12000-15000. ***Collection of Karen & Paul Dunlop, Photo © 1997 Papier Presse.***

This is an extraordinary and possibly unique paperweight from the Bacchus factory, and shows how adventurous they could be and how they were prepared to try anything that could further this art form. The paperweight is superbly overlaid in white glass with six side facets and a top window, with smaller facets cut around the base. The motif is made from five layers of different colored glass, which is then cooled and cut on a wheel to show the individual colors in what appears to be a Christmas weight with holly leaves and berries. This cutting is often described as "intaglio." The weight is then reheated to allow a final gather of clear glass to be added. This encasing technique was the most difficult process in paperweight production and rarely tried or perfected by any of the paperweight makers of the last century. To allow a paperweight to cool, engrave and deeply cut the surface, and then reheat the weight to a temperature that will allow another gather of molten glass to be added to the body of the paperweight, is a superb achievement. This is the only known example of this type from Bacchus, and was almost certainly a test piece. The skill and difficulty needed to make this a successful weight was so extreme that this weight is almost certainly unique.

Bacchus "Sodden Snow," c. 1850. Dia 3.45". $4500-5500. ***Collection of Karen & Paul Dunlop, Photo © 1997 Papier Presse.***

A spaced concentric "sodden snow" paperweight with canes appearing between the "snow" that have been squeezed into "bow ties." This was probably accidental and not a deliberate attempt at a "bow tie," but all the same a good likeness. The canes are all complex and show a good range of colors, including the lovely lilacs and soft pale greens. Several canes are made up of thirty or so smaller rods, and are complex to the extreme.

Bacchus Faceted Close Pack, c. 1850. Dia. 3". $3000-4000. *Courtesy of Mr. and Mrs. Richard Giles.*

An unusual six-sided close pack with a good selection of colorful cogs, tubes, and complex canes, all on a gently curved cushion. On the top of this piece is a shallow indentation about 1/16" deep. I have no idea of its purpose, nor do the owners of this lovely piece.

Profile of Faceted Close Pack. Height 2".

The cushion set-up of the canes can be seen reaching to the base of this piece. The outside row of blue and dark blue tube canes are drawn beneath to form a basket. The base is ground nearly flat.

Bacchus with Three Color Victoria Heads. Height 2.1". Dia. 3.75".$2500-3000. *Courtesy of Mr. & Mrs. Richard Giles.*

Three Victoria Silhouette canes, each on a different colored background, make this paperweight special. Two white heads are set into grounds of deep purple and dark blue, and one is colored dark green on a white ground. The large canes that make up this close pack are surrounded by a row of pink and white tubes which are drawn under the base to the centre, leaving a rough pontil mark. This is probably an early piece from the Bacchus glasshouse, as the quality of finish and cane work is not of the highest standard expected in a Bacchus paperweight.

Bacchus Four Row Concentric. c. 1850. Height 2.25". Dia. 3". $1500-2000. *Courtesy of Bill Volkman.*

Complex canes, tubes, and cogs make up the rows surrounding the unusual Victoria Head cane which looks as though it was slightly twisted while being drawn out. The canes are drawn to a nice finish on the base.

Bacchus Magnum Four Row Concentric with Torsade, c. 1850. Height 2.4". Dia. 3.7". $10,000-12,000. *Courtesy of Bill Volkman*

The torsade has been perfectly positioned around the base of the cane set-up to give the appearance of a "posy of flowers." The delicate canes blend into one another expertly, with a "rogue" cane just visible in the blue row, as a white centre to a single blue and white tube cane. The base of the weight has been ground perfectly flat.

Bacchus Close pack with Red and White Torsade, c. 1850. Height 2.2". Dia. 3.3". $4000-5000. *Courtesy of Bill Volkman.*

The torsade makes this weight very rare. The torsade technique was very difficult to master and rarely attempted. Although this paperweight uses simple cog and tube canes, the torsade makes it a very desirable and sought-after weight.

Bacchus Close Pack, c. 1850. Height 2.1". Dia. 3.4". $4000-5000. ***Courtesy of Bill Volkman.***

An excellent selection of small and large canes in deep and pastel colors. Most of the canes are easily recognizable as Bacchus and these close packs are ideal for identifying Bacchus paperweights. The outer canes are drawn to a fine finish on the base.

Bacchus Five Row Concentric, c. 1850. Height 2.2". Dia. 3.3". $3000-4000. ***Courtesy of Bill Volkman.***

A fine concentric set-up around a very large central feature cane that is encased in a thick layer of red and then white glass. The complex canes are all tightly packed together to prevent slippage. The outer row has been drawn to the centre of the base leaving a small window and ground pontil.

Bacchus Four Row Concentric, c. 1850. Height 2.25". Dia. 3.2". $4000-5000. ***Courtesy of Bill Volkman.***

The central cluster of complex canes makes this a very superior concentric. All the rows are made from clusters of simple canes that have been gathered together to make distinctive groupings. The central group of canes has among them a rarely seen black honeycomb cane. The rows of canes are so tightly packed together that they give the appearance of a carpet ground. The base is concave and finely finished, with a basal ring of only 1/16".

Bacchus Four Row Concentric, c. 1850. Height 2.2". Dia 3.3". $2250-2750. *Courtesy of Bill Volkman.*

This is a very colorful paperweight, but although it has a very well-made central cane the rest of the set-up lets it down, due to slippage of the other rows. The rows have been packed out with other canes but most of the canes look to be slightly distorted and poorly made.

Bacchus Four Row Concentric, c. 1850. Height 2.1". Dia. 3.4". $3500-4500. *Courtesy of Bill Volkman.*

The use of white ruffle canes provides a perfect contrast to deeper colored lilacs and reds, as seen in this lovely example. The red and lilac tubes are only simply made canes, but are shown to great effect when placed next to the white ruffles. The encased ruffle in the centre is delicately made between layers of white glass, with the encasing layer pulled down into a funnel to give the effect of a flower head.

Bacchus Five Row Concentric, c. 1850. Height 2.2". Dia. 3.3". $4000-5000. *Courtesy of Bill Volkman.*

Beautifully made with the rows all perfectly placed with no slippage. This is achieved by matching the canes by size and tightly packing them into the set-up ring; carelessness at this stage spoils the end result. The base is as well made as the crown.

Bacchus Five Row Concentric, c. 1850. Height 2.1". Dia. 3.4". $4000-5000. *Courtesy of Bill Volkman.*

The central feature cane is made from approximately fifty small tube and cog canes, bundled together and drawn out to make this extraordinary cane. This complex cane will enhance the value of any paperweight it is included in. The weight has a fine finish to the base with the outer rows of deep purple canes drawn to the centre with the pontil removed by grinding.

Bacchus Five Row Concentric, c. 1850. Height 2.3". Dia. 3.5". $4000-5000. *Courtesy of Bill Volkman.*

A fine white ruffle centres this nice paperweight from Bacchus. The next row has red and white tubes that has two odd canes with white stamens in the centres. Is this another worker telling us he made this weight? The base is finished with the outer row of canes drawn to a small porthole in the centre.

Bacchus Five Row Concentric, c. 1850. Height 2.2". Dia. 3.4". $4000-5000. *Courtesy of Bill Volkman.*

A central cluster of yellow canes are surrounded by a row of extremely complex red and white canes encased in a coat of red glass. The next row of blue and green canes are as equally complex, having cogs and tubes encased in a clear glass to hold them all together.

Bacchus Close Pack, c. 1850. Height 2.2". Dia. 3.3". $3500-4500. *Courtesy of Bill Volkman.*

Pale mint green surrounds most of the strongly colored canes in this close pack. The majority of the canes are well known cogs and ruffles, but a very rare honeycomb cane can be seen with careful viewing.

Bacchus Sodden Snow Close Pack, c. 1850. Height 2.2". Dia. 3.3". $4000-5000. *Courtesy of Bill Volkman.*

A good selection of canes in pastel shades all sit softly embedded in the sodden snow white glass that gives the appearance of cotton wool.

Bacchus Five Row Concentric, c. 1850. Height 2.3". Dia. 3.6". $4000-5000. *Courtesy of Bill Volkman.*

A well presented concentric until we get near the centre. Three "sodden snow" canes have been placed in the centre of the weight which totally spoils the continuity of the rows. What the glassworker was trying to achieve with this technique, I cannot imagine. The base has been perfectly finished to the centre.

Bacchus Four Row Concentric, c. 1850. Height 2.3". Dia. 3.4". $3750-4500. *Courtesy of Bill Volkman.*

A superb example of a concentric weight. The canes sit in almost perfect symmetry around a well constructed central cane. The rows of canes are slightly splayed to look like a flower bouquet. The use of the soft pistachio greens in the outer rows shows harmony of color. As you would imagine with a paperweight of this quality, the base is finished with a high degree of skill, the cane ends are drawn to the centre and left in a perfect porthole circle.

Bacchus Five Row Concentric, c. 1850. Height 2.2". Dia. 3.2". $4500-5000. *Courtesy of Bill Volkman.*

A good concentric with the central floret encased in a tube of blue glass and a white sleeve. The canes are of a simple construction, but packed in tightly to make this a desirable piece.

Bacchus Close Pack with Silhouette Canes. Height 2.3". Dia. 3.4". $3000-4000. *Courtesy of Bill Volkman.*

There are six Victoria Head Silhouettes to enhance this paperweight, with the further attraction of "oak" leaf canes. The weight is nicely put together with mainly ruffles, cogs, and tube canes.

Bacchus Concentric Bouquet with Torsade, c. 1850. Height 2.2". Dia. 3.5". $10,000-11,000. *Courtesy of Bill Volkman.*

The Latticinio red and white spiral torsade was perfected at the Bacchus glassworks to a very high degree of skill; it is doubtful whether a finer composition from this glassworks will ever be discovered. The pink and white lacy canes are set around a large flower head also made frpm delicate clear and white ruffles. A "rogue" cane is present in the pink row of canes to identify the maker.

Bacchus Five Row Concentric, c. 1850. Height 2.3". Dia. 3.5". $4500-5000. *Courtesy of Bill Volkman.*

More than twenty canes have been gathered together to make this central motif; each individual part of this amazing cane has been miniaturized by reheating the cane bundle and drawing the soft cane out to reduce it in size.

Base of Bacchus Concentric Bouquet with Torsade.

A wide basal ring can be seen on the bottom of this weight, which is in perfect condition, with no bruises or scratches to detract from its beauty. The cane ends are drawn in to a small porthole and then ground to a slight concavity.

Bacchus Five Row Concentric, c. 1850. Height 2.3". Dia. 3.4". $4000-4500. ***Courtesy of Bill Volkman.***

The central feature cane is made from grouping together normal sized canes, and reducing them in size by drawing out after reheating. These combination canes are a distinctive feature from Bacchus and can be a means of identification in their paperweights. The weight has the outer row of canes drawn to the centre of the base and lightly ground.

Bacchus Four Row Concentric, c. 1850. Height 2.2". Dia. 3.3". $4000-4500. ***Courtesy of Bill Volkman.***

The combination of the cane colors makes this a paperweight to be desired. The soft greens and pinks around the centre cane makes a pretty bouquet of flowers. The canes are all set very precisely and drawn to a small centre porthole on the base.

Bacchus Four Row Concentric, c. 1850. Height 2.3". Dia. 3.5". $4500-5000. ***Courtesy of Bill Volkman.***

The central cane is made from lacy white ruffle canes encased in a thick layer of dark blue, with a white outer tube of glass. Complex yellow and a row of rarely seen brown tubes with a complex centre are featured in this striking paperweight. The outer row is a very complex mixture of tubes and ruffles, all shown in miniature.

Bacchus Sodden Snow Spaced Concentric. Height 2.1". Dia 3.5". $3000-4000. *Courtesy of Bill Volkman.*

The millefiori canes look as though they are slowly sinking into the "snow." The canes have slipped when the "snow" glass has been lowered onto the cane set-up. Although these "sodden snow" paperweights are quite rare, this does not appear to be of the best quality, and may have been a test piece.

Bacchus Patterned Sodden Snow, c. 1850. Height 2.3". Dia. 3.3". $6000-7000. *Courtesy of Bill Volkman.*

A very attractive set of canes in this "snow" paperweight, sitting nicely on the surface, with the outer garland of canes drawn to the centre of the base and finished off very neatly. Although not always visible in the photographs, all "sodden snow" paperweights have the outer row drawn down and under to the centre of the base.

Bacchus Patterned Sodden Snow, c. 1850. Height 2.1". Dia. 3.4". $7000-8000. *Courtesy of Bill Volkman.*

This is an excellent example of the "sodden snow" paperweight, with good groups of canes that have remained in place when being encased in the "snow" glass. The techniques involved in the encasing process must have been very difficult, hence the rarity of these pieces.

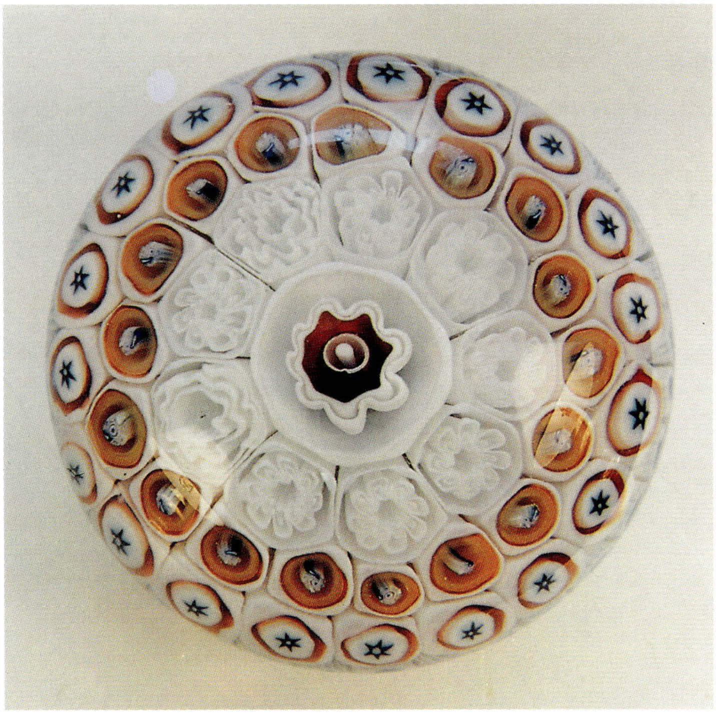

Bacchus Four Row Concentric, c. 1850. Height 2.4". Dia. 3.6". $5000-6000. *Courtesy of Bill Volkman.*

A perfectly constructed concentric in the unusual light brown and white color. This unusual color combination makes the weight quite special and rare. The pure white ruffle canes are set around the large and colorful red flower head, which is encased in clear glass and then a white tube.

Bacchus Four Row Concentric, c. 1850. Height 2.8". Dia. 3.7". $4500-5000. *Courtesy of Bill Volkman.*

A shield cane centres this lovely pink and white weight. The complex canes are well made and positioned to great effect. The unusual canes around the centre are bundles of blue and white cog canes, with approximately thirty or more in each bundle. In this row can be seen another "rogue" cane.

Bacchus Paneled Paperweight. c. 1850. Height 2.1". Dia 3.4". $7000-8000. *Courtesy of Bill Volkman.*

The blue and pink shield canes are circled by complex pink and green canes; the green, and pink tube canes then divide the weight into four parts. This design is unique among Bacchus paperweights and makes for a stunning weight. The base is almost as good as the crown, drawn down and under, the outer row of canes reaching the centre of the base to a small porthole, with the pontil lightly removed.

Bacchus Five Row Concentric, c. 1850. Height 2.2". Dia 3.3". $4000-5000. *Courtesy of Bill Volkman.*

The central feature cane is a group of ordinary canes that have been miniaturized. The complex rows of yellow, brown, and olive colored canes are tightly packed to prevent slippage. The addition of this large central cane enhances the paperweights value by 20 percent or more.

Bacchus Four Row Concentric, c. 1850. Height 2.2". Dia 3.3". $4000-4500. *Courtesy of Bill Volkman.*

Using only two colors, Bacchus has created a stunning paperweight. All the canes are ruffles with the outer row of green and white tubes drawn down and under to the centre of the base.

Bacchus Five Row Concentric, c. 1850. Height 2.3". Dia. 3.4". $3750-4250. *Courtesy of Bill Volkman.*

The shield canes around the lacy white centre feature cane are of too many different sizes, and the next row has the same problem. This uneven matching of canes spoils the whole weight. The three outer rows are set together tightly, with evenly sized canes. The outer row of tube canes are drawn beneath the weight to finish finely.

Bacchus Six Row Concentric, c. 1850. Height 2.1". Dia. 3.5". $4000-5000. ***Courtesy of Bill Volkman.***

A large floret of red and white, encased in a thin tube, makes these centre canes from Bacchus quite special and a trademark cane of this glassworks. All the rows are comprised of complex canes, tightly packed together with the outer row of tube canes drawn beneath the weight.

Bacchus Five Row Concentric, c. 1850. Height 2.3". Dia. 3.4". $5000-6000. ***Courtesy of Bill Volkman.***

This paperweight is very precisely set. The complex canes are set around a large white floret, with a further row of very detailed "oak" leaf canes, to add variety to an already perfect weight.

Bacchus Four Row Concentric, c. 1850. Height 2.3". Dia. 3.3". $3750-4250. ***Courtesy of Bill Volkman.***

Simple red and white tubes surround the green ruffle central feature cane. The outer two rows have added interest in the complex centres of the canes; the blue hollow rods are encased in a white sheath.

Bacchus Concentric with Mushroom Centre, c. 1850. Height 2.4". Dia. 3.6". $16,000-18,000. *Courtesy of Bill Volkman.*

This is probably the finest antique English paperweight ever made, and may even qualify as the best ever concentric from a glassworks anywhere. The precision of the set-up is quite staggering, with a total of eleven rows of canes, including one row on the outside that cannot be seen in the photograph. This last row of tube canes is pulled beneath the weight to hide the cane ends and finish to a precise porthole. As I expected, the "rogue" cane sits in the row of pink and white ruffles, with only the black centre missing to distinguish it from the others in the row. This weight would have taken a considerable amount of time and planning; even with the canes already made and cut to length, it could still have taken two men several days to get the many stages involved to all come together. It would need an expert modern paperweight maker such as Saint Louis to explain the many different stages to complete a weight with this complexity. The canes in the central rows are pulled down to a mushroom shape, which can be seen when viewing the paperweight on an angle.

Bacchus Concentric with Torsade, c. 1850. Height 2.5". Dia. 3.5". $5000-6000. *Courtesy of Bill Volkman.*

Green and white ruffles make up this rare weight with a small red, white, and blue torsade sitting over the ground of canes. The torsade lies only just beneath the surface of the dome. The torsade of twisted cane doesn't quite harmonize with the green and white background, but the weight is still a prized addition to anyone's collection.

Bacchus Concentric with Red and White Torsade. c. 1850. Height 2.3". Dia. 3.5". $10,000-11,000. *Courtesy of Bill Volkman.*

A superbly formed torsade surrounds this special and very rare paperweight from Bacchus. The red and white strips of glass encase a twist of white, almost translucent latticinio. The cane set-up of pale blue and thinly made ruffle canes add a delicate nature to the whole weight. A perfect paperweight and very highly prized among collectors

Bacchus Encased Basket of Flowers, c. 1850. Height 2.9". Dia. 3.6". $18,000-20,000. *Courtesy of Bill Volkman.*

This very unique creation from Bacchus demonstrates their willingness to experiment in this art form. Having mastered the art of paperweight making, this glasshouse would surely have gone on to create even more adventurous pieces had the paperweight market been sustainable and not gone into decline after the Bacchus company had just got started in the paperweight business. This paperweight would have almost certainly been made in the late 1850s, as it demonstrates the technique of encasing the paperweight after the cutting process had been applied. The paperweight is made as a normal weight, which is then completely covered in two layers of different colors, in this case purple and then white. The paperweight is then allowed to cool, and is then cut on an abrasive wheel to remove part of the overlay to form the basket. After polishing, the weight is placed in an annealing oven to gently bring the paperweight back up to a sufficiently high temperature to allow another gather of clear glass to be added. This process may have taken up to forty-eight hours, as reheating the paperweight too quickly causes stress within the glass with fractures and cracking as a result. The small canes used in this "basket of flowers" are simple cogs, tubes, and stars, but if this type of paperweight had proved to be successful, and economical to produce, then we can only imagine the canes that could have been used in further "flower baskets."

Base of Bacchus Flower Basket.

Profile of Bacchus Encased Flower Basket.

The profile shows the bottom of the basket sitting on a thick gather of glass. The base has been ground flat, with a large window cut in the overlay to allow the canes to be seen, which have been drawn together to a small porthole in the centre of the base. As this was a "one off" or test piece, the weight is not 100 percent perfect, but the skill, time, and patience needed to have achieved this piece is commendable.

Bacchus Blue and White Torsade Concentric. Height 2.4". Dia. 3.7". $10,000-12,000. *Courtesy of Bill Volkman.*

A magnificent "posy of flowers" set within a blue and white torsade. The delicate flower head centre cane is surrounded by a row of crimped tube canes with a central stamen. Green open canes with two rows of pure white open canes complete this superb combination of color and artistry. The canes are drawn to the centre of the perfectly flat base.

Bacchus Three Row Concentric, c. 1850. Height 2.3". Dia. 3.5". $7000-8000. *Courtesy of Bill Volkman.*

As a central feature cane, they don't come any bigger or better than this superbly crafted beauty from Bacchus. The cane was made by adding layers of clear and white glass alternately, then encasing in a blue and white tube. It was very rare for Bacchus to make more than one paperweight of the same pattern, as only one or two pieces have been found to be the same as another. Although they used the same canes in many paperweights, they all tend to show many differences in design, color, and construction. This central cane may be unique and made especially for this weight. The other rows have well known shield and ruffle canes with the outer row of tube canes drawn to the centre of the base and precisely finished to a small porthole. On the edge of this porthole can be found a small "rogue" cane. The maker of this weight did not wish to spoil his creation with an odd cane, so he hid it underneath the paperweight. It may be that the glassmaker was also hiding his signature cane from the management, as some of these "rogue" canes can be difficult to find and usually found only with the aid of a strong magnifying glass.

Base of Bacchus Three Row Concentric.

Bacchus glassmakers were experts at finishing off the base. Once the technique had been mastered, the base can be as good and as interesting as many paperweight domes. The "rogue" cane seen in the porthole is testament to one man's skill. The cane he used to pull down is a shield cane in perfect miniature.

Bacchus Concentric with All Over Faceting, c. 1850. Height 2.2". Dia. 3.4". $4500-5000. ***Courtesy of Bill Volkman.***

The central feature cane is made from simple stars encased in white glass and then picked up with dark blue glass, the same way a paperweight is made. These canes were only loosely packed and some slippage can be seen. The rest of the paperweight is well made, with the faceting adding to its value.

Bacchus Concentric with All Over Faceting, c. 1850. Height 2.2". Dia. 3.4". $5000-6000. ***Courtesy of Bill Volkman.***

The centre cane is similar to a previous example, but this one has a green tube encasing it, with a selection of small open tubes as stamens. The all over faceting is an attractive addition to this weight, which has five rows of complex canes in amber and reds. The outer tube canes are drawn to the centre of the base.

Base of Concentric with All Over Faceting.

The base of this weight is very well made, with the deeply colored purple outer row of canes drawn to a porthole in the centre of the base.

Bacchus White Carpet Ground, c. 1850. Height 2.3". Dia. 3.5". $4000-5000. *Courtesy of Bill Volkman.*

A delightful carpet of white ruffle canes surrounds a large red and white feature cane. Carpet grounds are quite rare from the Bacchus works and only three or four are known. A "rogue" cane can be seen on the outer row on this weight, but is not visible in this photograph.

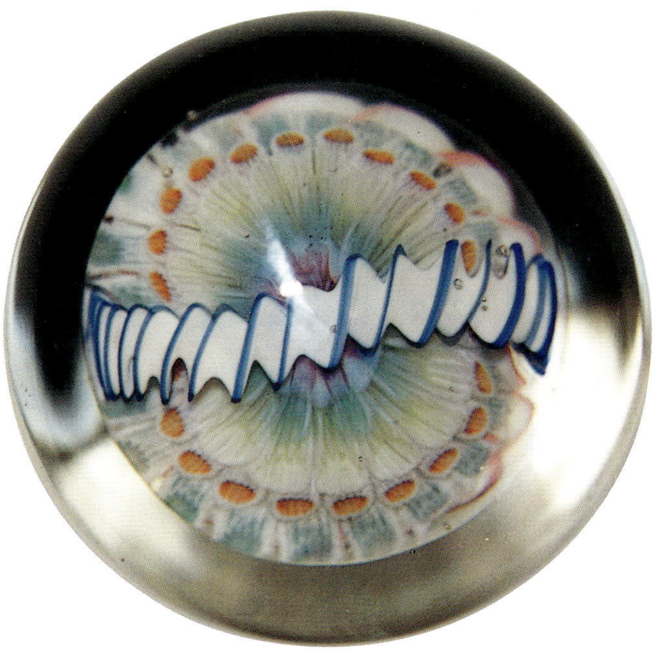

Bacchus Basket Paperweight. Height 2.4". Dia. 3.5". $5000-6000. *Courtesy of Bill Volkman.*

This is possibly another unique paperweight from Bacchus. The extra time involved in creating these special pieces would mean that they were certainly not production pieces, and were more likely to have been made on the glassworker's own time to test his skill and technique. The canes used in this weight are very soft in color and have a "feathery" quality to them. The canes are almost translucent and have been drawn outwards to form a mushroom shape. The blue and white torsade always adds to a paperweight's interest and value.

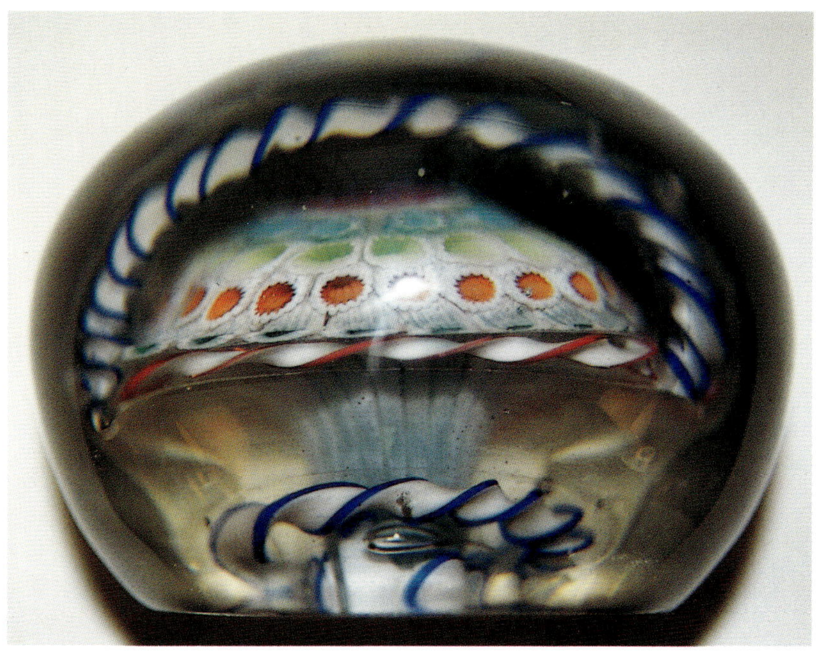

Profile of Bacchus Basket Paperweight.

Not content with a torsade handle to the basket, Bacchus went a little further in their experimenting and added a further three beneath the weight. The mushroom stalk has two blue and white torsades attached to, and around, the stem, with another red and white just beneath the mushroom cap. The base is hollow ground with the canes finishing in the centre of the weight. The base rests on a 1/4" basal rim.

Bacchus Close Pack with All Over Faceting. Height 2.2". Dia. 3.3". $4000-5000. *Courtesy of Bill Volkman.*

A good mixture of stars and cogs in this paperweight with all over circular facets. The base is slightly concave with the pontil ground off.

Bacchus Five Row Concentric, c. 1850. Height 2.2". Dia. 3.4". $3500-4000. *Courtesy of Bill Volkman.*

Three rows of tightly packed complex canes are on the outside of this concentric, but a little slippage amongst the green ruffle canes has allowed the middle two rows to move as well. It would seem that the smaller the canes used, the less slippage. The Bacchus Glassworks opted to use bigger than average canes to display their beautiful cane designs. Even if the canes have moved a little, this is still a valuable and treasured paperweight.

Bacchus Four Row Concentric, c. 1850. Height 2.3". Dia. 3.4". $4000-4500. *Courtesy of Bill Volkman.*

A shield cane centres this paperweight, which has a little untidiness to the cane set-up but has two rows of complex ruffle canes to add interest and desirability. The base is finished in typical Bacchus style.

Bacchus Five Row Concentric, c. 1850. Height 2.3". Dia. 3.4". $4000-5000. *Courtesy of Bill Volkman.*

A well-made central ruffle encased in a blue and white tube centres this good concentric. One row is composed of a bunch of white rods in a red lined white tube. The rows are all neatly held together with the outer row of tube canes, drawn down and beneath the weight to the centre of the base.

Bacchus Magnum Mushroom Concentric with Torsade, c. 1850. Height 2.6". Dia. 3.9". $10,000-11,000. *Courtesy of Bill Volkman.*

This stunning magnum from Bacchus has the central flower bouquet drawn down to a mushroom shape beneath the weight. The lacy white and green ruffle canes are made with a very thin coating of color, to make the canes almost transparent. The weight is in a pristine condition, and has been a treasured item in the hands of collectors for nearly 150 years.

Bacchus Five Row Concentric, c. 1850. Height 2.1". Dia. 3.3". $3750-4250. *Courtesy of Bill Volkman.*

A large red and white crimped cane in a white tube is a typical central feature from Bacchus. These large canes, when well made, are a specialty of this glasshouse and help in the identification process. This central cane blends nicely in this weight, with only one slightly out-of-position cane to spoil what is almost the perfect concentric.

Bacchus Four Row Concentric, c. 1850. Height 2.1". Dia. 3.3". $3500-4000. *Courtesy of Bill Volkman.*

Only four rows of canes are found in this colorful creation from Bacchus, using a simple row of open canes and crimps. The surprise lies in the outer row. This row is made from joining together over twenty-five cogs and tubes with the odd complex cane, and then encasing all in a white tube to make one of the Bacchus specialty canes. To find one in a paperweight is always a delight, but this weight has a complete row of nineteen. The barely visible row of tube canes on the edge of the weight are pulled down and beneath the weight to the centre of the base to create a fine finish.

Bacchus Five Row Concentric, c. 1850. Height 2.2". Dia. 3.5". $4500-5000. *Courtesy of Bill Volkman.*

Four rows of complex canes with an outer row of cogs that are drawn beneath the weight to the centre. The unusual mustard colored canes encase a small complex centre. It is possible that a darker colored cane would be more suitable in this otherwise dark paperweight. The use of so many dark rows is not typical of Bacchus, but it would seem they were never shy of trying something a little different.

Bacchus Five Row Concentric, c. 1850. Height 2.3". Dia. 3.4". $4000-4500. *Courtesy of Bill Volkman.*

All five rows are neatly packed together around this lovely central white ruffle cane. The red tube canes have two stamens in two of the canes, could this be someone else signing his work? These two odd canes certainly add interest to a stunning paperweight.

Bacchus Five Row Concentric, c. 1850. Height 2.3". Dia. 3.5". $3000-4000. ***Courtesy of Bill Volkman.***

Most of the canes are quite simply constructed, and this weight may be from the early days of the Bacchus production. It is well finished on the base with the outer rows drawn down and under to the centre.

Bacchus Five Row Concentric, c. 1850. Height 2.3". Dia. 3.4". $3750-4250. ***Courtesy of Bill Volkman.***

The large centre cane has a row of quite common pink and white canes that comprise a gathering of fourteen small cog canes, with a single white rod in the centre. The other rows are also of the complex variety, with one row made from very small rods encased in a blue lining, and then in "sodden snow." This glass cane has an almost gray appearance.

Bacchus Five Row Concentric, c. 1850. Height 2.3". Dia. 3.5". $4000-4500. Courtesy of Bill Volkman.

This weight has a superb row of complex blue and pink plus green and white ruffle canes interspersed around the bottom edge and sandwiched between two rows of white ruffle canes. This color combination would have made this a visually spectacular paperweight, but the glassworker has placed two rows of dark blue and brown canes which spoil the delicate nature of the outer rows. A desirable paperweight, just for the pink and green canes.

Bacchus Six Row Concentric, c. 1850. Height 2.3". Dia. 3.5". $3750-4250. *Courtesy of Bill Volkman.*

A good concentric with three rows of star canes and two other rows with blue and white and red and white complex canes. One row of tube canes on the lower edge has been pulled down and under to the centre of the weight to a fine finish.

Bacchus Five Row Concentric, c. 1850. Height 2.2". Dia. 3.5". $3500-4000. *Courtesy of Bill Volkman.*

This weight has two rows of canes to match the previous paperweight. Bacchus only very rarely made two weights identical, which may have occurred by chance rather than by design.

Bacchus Five Row Concentric, c. 1850. Height 2.3". Dia. 3.6". $3750-4250. *Courtesy of Bill Volkman.*

This paperweight has a complex and lacy ruffled centre cane, strikingly set in a dark blue ground and encased in a thin white tube. A row of hollow brown complex canes are placed next to a very complex row of canes on the edge of the weight, which are made from many small rods of dark blue and mint green. The unseen row of tube canes on the outside edge are drawn to the centre of the weight and finished precisely.

Bacchus Five Row Concentric, c. 1850. Height 2.3". Dia. 3.3". $4000-4500. *Courtesy of Bill Volkman.*

This paperweight has three rows of canes in common with the previous two weights; even sharing these same features, the weights have enough variations to make each one an individual and desirable paperweight. This weight has a splendid central feature cane of pink and pale blue tubes, grouped together to make a single large cane.

Bacchus Six Row Concentric, c. 1850. Height 2.2". Dia. 3.4". $4000-4500. *Courtesy of Bill Volkman.*

Over forty canes comprise the amazing feature cane in the centre of this well-made paperweight. Using slightly smaller canes, the maker has formed the set-up without any slippage in the other rows. The unseen outer row of tube canes are drawn to the centre of the base and finished with a small porthole.

Bacchus Five Row Concentric, c. 1850. Height 2.3". Dia. 3.5". $3750-4250. *Courtesy of Bill Volkman.*

A red and white central flower cane sits in a tube of white glass pulled down to a cone shape. The whole weight is tightly packed with canes that are slightly leaning outwards to give the impression of a flower head, perhaps of a pompom Dahlia or Chrysanthemum. The concentric millefiori paperweight tries to imitate "flowers that clothe the meadows," and of the many who have tried, Bacchus has come the closest.

Chapter Four

Islington Glass Works

Sheepcote Street, Birmingham, England

In 1803 Owen Johnson founded a glasshouse making all kinds of flint glass wares, cut and fancy. In 1818 he took a partner named Rice Harris. The business flourished and was still producing glass until the 1850s. In 1849 they exhibited flint glass wares at the Bingley Hall, Birmingham, and again at the 1851 Great Exhibition held at the Crystal Palace, London.

Very little is known about the history and products produced by this factory. *Kellys Post Office and Address Book* lists them as "Flint Glass Producers," Sheepcote Street.

It is known that they produced paperweights, and very fine weights at that, although there are only a few known examples. One is at present in the Bergstrom Mahler Museum, Neenah, Wisconsin, and is illustrated in the book on the Museum collection[1]. Another two are held by private collectors. The one held by the museum is a superb close pack containing a tremendous variety of canes, including arrow, star, whorl, and a small cane, shaped like a propeller. Other canes include the silhouette of a draught horse, with the black horse set in a block of white glass. Set in amongst these lovely canes is a white oblong block with the initials IGW in black. The weight is 2.7 inches in diameter. Another weight is illustrated in the book *Identifying Antique Paperweights*[2] and shows a very rare cane called a honeycomb. This is a combination of twenty-five hollow tubes set in a square, encased in clear glass, and surrounded by eighteen cross canes. The two weights in the private collections are close packs, and are described in the photo captions. These four paperweights show a substantial variety of simple and quite complex canes.

Such variety can only mean that all these different cane designs were meant for a substantial production of paperweights, and that there must be quite a few more survivors from this factory. By asking a few collecting colleagues for information in a newsletter, one "survivor" turned up, much to my delight. It is possible, because of the similarity between Baccarat close packed and Islington close packed weights, especially if they are not signed with that distinctive IGW cane, that by checking for the Islington canes I have mentioned you may find a mis-attributed, extremely rare paperweight.

Many English paperweights turn up in the Midlands area of England; the Birmingham and surrounding areas have been a rich source for paperweights at flea and antique markets, and have been the basis of my own collection of English paperweights. I hope my continuing search will eventually be rewarded, and that my own collection will be honoured with an IGW weight. I would be very interested to hear from anyone who owns or knows the whereabouts of any more Islington paperweights.

Profile of Islington Close Pack with Cross. Height 2".

The dome is a low cushion, similar in shape to the Bacchus weights, with the canes reaching about half way to the top of the weight. The sides curve steeply to the base with the outside row of canes roughly drawn to the centre.

Base of Islington Close Pack with Cross.

The base was a surprise to me, as I was not expecting to find an English weight with the base ground totally flat. The IGW paperweight in the Bergstrom Mahler Museum has a slightly concave base. The cane ends are drawn in towards the centre, but not too precisely. The base also shows traces of pitting in the glass with a clay-like substance in the indentations. The whole weight is encased in a heavy coating of glass. This makes the dimensions the same as the weight in the Bergstrom Mahler Museum.

Opposite page:
Islington Close Pack with Cross, c. 1850. *Courtesy of Colin McCallien.*

It is not possible to place a value on this weight, as Islington weights virtually never appear for sale at auction with the proper attribution. This is probably one of the rarest paperweights known to collectors, with only four examples known to the author. The weight itself is not of the highest quality, but the individual canes show that the factory could and did produce weights of a superior nature. The central feature is a "cross" with upraised arms, described by the owner as possibly being a representation of the Catholic "Trinity." The cross is formed with blackberry type canes, similar in construction to the Clichy moss ground cane. The black cane has white stardust rods set into the ground. Sitting next to the cross are two arrow head canes, black arrows on white, with a complex red and white centre. A small propeller cane can be seen at the bottom left, white on green. The other canes filling in the paperweight are mainly white stardust canes; this stardust cane seems to be the basis for most of the canes to be seen in this weight. Red and white and blue and white stardust canes can also be observed. The outstanding feature of this paperweight is the black IGW on a white oblong tablet. Thank goodness this manufacturer took the trouble to sign their weights, without which this weight could only be allocated to the page on "unknowns," or "probably English."

Islington Glass Works, c. 1850. Height 1.75". Dia. 2.7". *Courtesy of Bergstrom-Mahler Museum, Neenah, Wisconsin, USA.*

The Bergstrom-Mahler has one of the finest collections of paperweights in the world, with the added attraction of one of the rarest weights known to the paperweight collector. The canes in this Islington paperweight are also quite unique to this glasshouse. The black draught horse, propeller cane, and blackberry type canes have never been seen in any other weight. Anyone lucky enough to find a weight with any of these canes can be certain it was made by the Islington Glassworks. The base is ground almost flat, with an almost imperceptible concavity, to leave a very small basal ring. The black draught horse silhouette is finely made with sharply outlined features, and the black arrow head canes are also possibly unique to this factory. The use of black glass for several of the canes is also quite a distinctive feature of this glassworks.

Islington Glassworks Close Pack with Horse Silhouettes, c. 1850. Height 1.8". Dia. 2.7". ***Courtesy of a Private Collector.***

This Islington weight has a collection of canes that have been made with skill and precision. The colors are sharp and the complex canes are unusual and well defined. Included among them are several whorl canes that start in the centre with an open end similar to the French Saint Louis whorls, except that this one has a star cane in the centre. The draught horse silhouettes are an added bonus in this exquisite paperweight from Islington Glassworks.

Profile of Islington Close Pack.

Base of Islington Close Pack.

The canes are drawn in, with the base being ground flat.

Close-up of Islington Close Pack.

Five draught horses, complex canes with propeller centres, star dust canes, and other simply made complex canes combine to make this a special paperweight.

Chapter Five

John Kilner

Wakefield, Yorkshire, England

John Kilner (1792-1857) established a glasshouse in 1829 for the commercial production of green glass bottles and jars. After a few years, Kilner and his business partners decided to go their own ways. John Kilner set up with his son in the town of Wakefield, which had a plentiful supply of all the raw materials needed to produce glass close at hand. The Yorkshire area has an abundance of coal and good quality sand and potash. The business was then known as John Kilner & Son. In the 1830s, his younger son joined the business, which was retitled John Kilner & Sons. In 1844 John must have retired as the business was renamed Kilner Brothers.

The firm prospered throughout the nineteenth century to become a major producer of commercial glass of all types. The range of goods included jars, bottles, and carboys of various sizes. The company exported world-wide and were so prolific in the production of jars that the name "Kilner jars" entered the English language.

The paperweight side of the business must have been at a considerable level, judging by the amount of doorstops, table ornaments, and paperweights that are still readily available at antique fairs and auctions today. It has been said that the green glass dumps were so common in the nineteenth and early twentieth centuries that workers lined their garden paths with them. There were many other glasshouses in the Yorkshire area, with sixteen in and around the Wakefield area alone. Production of dumps and paperweights were probably made by these other factories as well, but it is the Kilner glasshouse that produced the majority of the better quality weights and ornaments.

Signed weights that are signed J. Kilner were produced from the 1829-30 period, and must qualify as the earliest of the English paperweights. These early weights were probably used as advertising aids and given away to customers. Many of the smaller weights and ornaments have been made with considerable skill and care. The glassworkers, although mainly producing commercial products, have shown a certain amount of artistry in the structuring of the weights and ornaments. Most of the prized pieces have the same silver foil flowers, or flowers that seem to be made from thousands of tiny bubbles, but all emerging on stalks from the same type of flower pots. The flowers are all stylized convolvolus, which can be colored either pink or blue. Very rarely one can have a dash of yellow twist loosely threaded through. I have never seen any with a color other than the three mentioned here.

The majority of the most frequently found weights and doorstops are nothing more than green glass with elongated bubbles. Very little skill was needed to produce these end-of-the-day items, and most workers would have tried at sometime to make a doorstop for a family member or friend. These bubble weights are made by piercing the hot glass with a sharp steel rod, and when the rod is withdrawn from the glass a small amount of air is trapped inside. On reheating, expansion produces the teardrops that are seen in most doorstops. The size varies little, being around 5 or 6 inches tall, with paperweights showing more variation from 2.5 inches to 3.5 inches tall. The one consistency in this type of paperweight is the green glass coloring, with only a small variation of color between the many glass makers that must have made these items over many years.

All were made to enhance the worker's skills with glass, usually at the end of a production day, but it also proved to be a good opportunity to turn the waste glass into a profit, and many must have been sold at the height of paperweight popularity, around 1848-55. The quality of many pieces is extremely poor, having been hurriedly made with little thought for artistic content. This would explain the considerable mistreatment most of these items have received over the last hundred years or so. Being of little value at the time, the paperweights and doorstops have even been used as hammers. Any item that shows the bruises and indentations associated with severe misuse are not worth restoring, as the glass repair and regrinding shops that repair paperweights are very reluctant to regrind these pieces because the glass is extremely hard. A bruise that looks to be lying on the surface of the paperweight can sometimes be 0.25 of an inch deep and causes serious wear to the grinding wheel.

John Kilner Green Glass Paperweight with Convolvolus Flowers, c. 1829. Dia. 3". $600-700. *Author's Collection.*

This type of green glass paperweight was made from the same glass that was used to produce all manner of items used for the storage of wet and dry goods. The glass is of good quality and virtually free from striae and other impurities. Three convolvolus type flowers sit in a silver foil flower pot. The pot shows signs of stress marks and stretching. The foil has separated in several places due to cooling and reheating at the furnace. The flowers have pink centres, made from a single cane with an added thin layer of color. The cane is sliced thinly and laid on the foil to make a focal point. This weight is in excellent condition and it is quite rare to find one with no bruises. The weights and ornaments made by Kilners are the most prized of the green glass types and can command high prices, if signed. The artistic content in this paperweight is quite noticeable as the delicate foil inclusions must have been very difficult to handle. A steel rod is pressed down through the centres of the flowers to make the stems. Currently, signed Kilner weights are reaching considerable prices, with two being sold recently for $650 in England in 1997.

Base of Kilner Paperweight.

The base inscription dates the weight quite accurately. On this one it says, J KILNER MAKER, WAKEFIELD, and was made in 1829 when John Kilner worked without his son's involvement in the business. The name is impressed on a small green glass tablet approximately one inch in diameter, and is usually found only on the paperweight-sized pieces, which were possibly given away to advertise the company products and skills. I have never seen a signature tablet on a doorstop or table ornament. This tablet sets Kilners apart from the rest of the green glass doorstop makers of the North and the Midlands areas of England, as no other makers identified their products in this way. Tablets can be found on only a very few weights. I have seen many hundreds of green glass weights on my travels around the English antique fairs, and have only seen a total of six or seven with this signature tablet. One had a yellow twist of cane in it, but was badly damaged on the signature tablet leaving only a few letters of the name visible.

Profile of Kilner Paperweight. Height 3.125".

The profile is very distinctive and, unlike the majority of most other paperweights, it is very tall in relationship to its width. The weight balances on a base that has the sides reaching under the base, to the point where the paperweight seems top heavy resting on the tablet with the makers name impressed.

J.Kilner Single Foil Flower in Flowerpot, c. 1829. Height 3". Dia. 2.75". $200-250. *Private Collection.*

This paperweight has a single flower with seven silver foil petals, all emerging from a flowerpot on a short stalk from a silver foil vase. A tablet is attached to the base with the makers name impressed. J KILNER, MAKER, WAKEFIELD would be the whole inscription, but this weight has suffered considerable damage to the base and crown, and only a few letters are readable. With these few letters the weight can be dated to c. 1829. Despite its serious damage, the paperweight is rare and still collectible for its historic and datable history, being one of the first English paperweights to be made.

John Kilner Ovoid Table or Mantle Ornament, with Blue Foil Petals, c. 1830. Height 4.75". Dia. 3.5". $450-550. *Author's Collection.*

This was surely designed as a table or mantle ornament. It shows too much care and attention in the complicated manufacturing process to be used on the floor as a doorstop. A large piece, 4.75" tall, it has a single fourteen-petal flower head that fills the dome, and six smaller flowers arranged beneath the flower head. The larger flower has alternate blue and silver foil petals with a slight domed centre of opaque glass. The smaller flowers beneath are arranged on stalks in a vase with a foil surface. The stalks were made by pushing a steel rod into the hot viscous glass through the centres of the flowers, trapping a small amount of air inside; when encased in the final coating of glass, the air expands to form a bubble. This piece is not signed as with the Kilner paperweights, but it is probable that Kilners were the only glass house to use this foil method for petals, the other glasshouses opting for the easier method of rolling the glass in chalk or some other powder to make flowers. This ornament is in an extremely fine condition and has been appreciated and cared for by its previous owners over the last 150 years. There is no damage to the surface and only a small amount of detritus floating in the glass. The value of the piece is enhanced from the rest of the green glass items by the inclusion of the colored interspaced petals.

J. Kilner Ovoid Table Ornament with Silver Foil Petals, c. 1830. Height 5". Dia. 3.5". $400-500. *Author's Collection.*

The same size and form as the previous item but without the colored petals. The ornament is well made and very collectible. This is in a good condition without bruising and would be a valuable addition to anyone's collection.

If a piece is valuable, as with a signed Kilner, then the repair can be undertaken and can be worthwhile paying the extra for regrinding.

Green glass weights and doorstops have continued to be made up to the present. Even now it is possible to purchase a green glass doorstop or paperweight in pristine condition, as a glasshouse in Yorkshire continues to produce these popular items. The company is called Hartley Woods. This company sells the items as new, but inevitably these new products find their way onto the antique markets and are sold as Victorian Green Glass Dumps. A dealer may not be aware in some cases that the dump he is selling was only made a year or so ago, and the purchaser may think he has a bargain to find one in such good condition. One "Antique Centre" in the Cotswold's area of England, when told the asking price of $300 for a pair of nineteenth century matching doorstops that were almost certainly modern as not a single scratch on the base could be seen, replied that they were "from a good home and had been well looked after."

Six Petal Foil Weight. Height 3". Dia. 2.75". $350-450. ***Courtesy of Anne Anderson.***

Unlike a previous paperweight by Kilner, this one has only six petals; the flower is set in a flowerpot. The base is inscribed JOHN KILNER, WAKEFIELD.

J. Kilner Paperweight with Silver Foil Flower, c. 1830. Height 3.2". Dia. 3". $400-450. ***Courtesy of Anne Anderson.***

This has a single, six-petaled foil flower and flowerpot. The petals and flower pot show signs of stress caused by the heating and cooling processes of paperweight making. All foil inclusions in paperweights or ornaments show these stress marks; the foil is so thin as to be almost translucent. On the flower petals it is possible to see where the ends have burnt into holes, due to the molten glass being too hot when the petals were picked up off the marver plate. A rare collector's weight with just slight damage to the surface.

Base of Kilner Paperweight Showing Impressed Tablet with "J KILNER, WAKEFIELD"

This tablet made the paperweight unsteady and top-heavy, but the tablet dates the weight quite precisely to within a year of 1830 when John Kilner set up on his own account with no partners or family involved at this time. It is always a "find" to see one with the tablet and all the letters still readable, as this part of the weight is particularly prone to damage.

Kilner Swirl Weight, c. 1830. Height 3". Dia. 2.8". $300-400. ***Courtesy of Mr. & Mrs. Richard Giles.***

A paperweight with air bubbles swirled around inside this piece makes it different from other Kilner weights but relatively uninteresting.

Base of Kilner Weight.

The base of this weight has more interest than the unattractive crown. The impressed words J. KILNER WAKEFIELD add value to this collectible paperweight. The paperweight is in an almost new condition, with no bruises or scratches.

J.Kilner Table or Mantle Ornament with Eight Foil Flowers, c. 1830. Height 5.5". Dia. 3.5". $400-500. ***Courtesy of Anne Anderson.***

These items of green glass have always been called by collectors "dumps or doorstops;" as you can see from this example, this top-heavy doorstop would be next to useless holding open a heavy Victorian door. We can, therefore, rename these pieces "table or mantle ornaments," which is probably why they incorporated such well-made interiors. Doorstops are much cruder in construction and the pieces we see at the antique fairs nowadays show the kind of wear you would expect from something that has spent the last 150 years being bumped and banged by feet and doors and rolled around the floor. The foil flowers on this weight are well made and add a lightness to the heavy green glass. The eight flowers with pierced centres are set in a vase with a scalloped edge. The narrow waist and tapered form leaves it decidedly top-heavy, especially as the pontils were only broken off these pieces and never ground to remove the rough edges. This can leave a stump for the ornament to pivot on, and possibly be unbalanced. A sought-after collector's piece, in nice condition, and a prized possession. Many English collectors collect only these green glass examples, and collections only rarely appear at auction.

Chapter Six

Green Glass Doorstops

Unknown Makers in Yorkshire and the Midlands Area of England, 1830 to Present

Doorstops have been made in the Midland and Yorkshire areas of England since the start of commercial glassmaking. The Midlands is the central part of England, and covers such counties and towns with a glassmaking heritage as Stourbridge in Worcestershire, Birmingham in Warwickshire, and Wolverhampton in Staffordshire. In and around these counties and towns were established a multitude of firms producing domestic and commercial glass, which was exported throughout the British Empire during its heyday. In the Stourbridge area alone, as many as twelve glasshouses were in full production, employing most of the area's population in the 1870s.

With this vast production of glass came the wastage at the end of the working day. The glassworkers were encouraged in most factories to test their skills with this spare glass, usually on their own time. It was from this waste glass that the doorstop was born. The quality varied enormously, from a block of colored glass with no inclusions to superb pieces made by craftsmen who took immense pride in their work. It is these crafted pieces that have survived the test of time.

Doorstops with no artistic content would be used, abused, and discarded, whereas the better made pieces would be cherished and cared for as ornamental objects. The Yorkshire area around Wakefield had an even greater concentration of glassworks, with sixteen firms listed around the 1870s. Among these were the Kilner family, whose production was immense even by today's mass production standards. The style of the doorstop varied little between different areas of the country, almost always a large mass of glass with bubbles or flowers in pots or vases. Color was rarely used, with only the signed Kilner pieces showing petals made from blue silver foil and the occasional pink centre of a flower. The green color varied only slightly and it is not possible to identify individual glasshouses by this color variation.

The decoration was achieved by rolling the hot glass in chalk or a similar substance on the marver plate. This marver would be a solid flat sheet of iron or steel on which the viscous glass could be rolled and pulled into the desired shape. The chalk is picked up by the glass when rolled in it; when reheated and covered by another layer of glass, the chalk oxidizes and forms tiny bubbles, giving a silvery shine to the petals. A substantial amount of patience and skill would be required to form the petals on certain of the three-dimensional, multi-layered flowers. These better quality pieces look very like the silver foil weights and ornaments attributed to John Kilner and family and are possibly variations made by them. Some however, are crudely made, full of striation and dirt and not attractive at all. Many have a clay inclusion of various motifs, including figures and a bunch of flowers. This inclusion is nearly always crudely made with no intention for commercial production. In a few, broken clay pies were inserted.

Doorstop, Nineteenth Century, Maker Unknown. Height 5". Dia. 3.4". $400-500. ***Author's Collection.***

A well-made doorstop, or ornament, that could have been made by Kilners. The set-up of the chalk flowers in a flowerpot is very similar to previous examples by the John Kilner factory. The artistic content is very much in evidence and must have been extremely difficult to perfect. The flowers have had a steel pin pushed through the centres to create the thin stems; this pin could be a thin tube, as a large bubble has been blown into the centres of the flower heads. A piece as complex as this one must have meant many journeys to the furnace to add layers of glass encapsulating the flowers and bubbles.

Paperweight, Nineteenth Century, Maker Unknown. Height 3.25". Dia. 3". $150-175. ***Author's Collection.***

A simple paperweight with one flower inside, but in nice condition and a very useful object in an 1830s household with draughty rooms. It is the ideal desk companion when windows are open and papers need securing.

Ovoid Doorstop, Nineteenth Century, Maker Unknown. Height 4.5". Dia. 3". $300-400. ***Author's Collection.***

This is a very common example, but well made with care. It is possible to see the different layers of glass that were added to encase the flowers at the three levels above the flower pot. After each powdered flower was collected from the marver, the pin was pushed into the centre of the flower to form the short stem; this pushing down into the very soft glass leaves the indentation for the next flower head and stalk to sit on.

Paperweight, Nineteenth Century, Maker Unknown. Height 3.3". Dia. 3". $200-250. *Author's Collection.*

A paperweight with a three-dimensional flower in a flower pot or vase. From the numbers of this type of paperweight seen on the English market, it is quite possible that many glasshouses did have production runs of them to satisfy a local market. They were cheap to make and affordable by the general populace. It must be remembered that in the mid-nineteenth century, everyone wrote letters to communicate, and some heavy item was needed on desks to hold down paper. A paperweight was decorative and pleasant to handle on a warm day.

Paperweight, Nineteenth Century. Height 3.25". Dia. 3.35". $150-175. *Author's Collection.*

This paperweight would be acceptable for use, had it not been for the very dirty flower head. This may be the result of an unclean marver; perhaps the worker forgot to wipe off the accumulated dust from the day's activities, or was just careless. Although it still has a value in the antiques trade, I do not see collectors fighting over this piece, and it would have to be priced at a level to entice a collector.

Doorstop, Nineteenth or Early Twentieth Century. Height 4.25". Dia. 3.1". $175-250. *Author's Collection.*

A crude version of earlier examples, made at an obscure glassworks by an unskilled worker. The elements are all there except the skill of the glassworker. The flower petals are loosely formed and are not attached to the stems. The bubbles near the centre of the flower heads do not look part of anything in particular, with no obvious pattern, and with many small pieces of detritus floating around. This is not a good collector's example, but still sold at nearly every antiques fair in England.

Doorstop, Nineteenth Century. Height 5". Dia. 3.25". $350-400. ***Courtesy of Anne Anderson.***

The most often encountered doorstops are the elongated bubble type. These can be seen at antique shops and fairs anywhere in England. Although very common they can command high prices if in good condition, as many people specialize in collecting this particular type of object. They are simply made by a steel rod or tube being pushed into the soft glass to form a multitude of bubbles. These tall heavy objects were made as doorstops and not as ornamental pieces.

Doorstop, Nineteenth Century. Height 4.75". Dia. 3.5". $400-450. ***Courtesy of Anne Anderson.***

The same as the previous piece but with a slight variation in color. It is impossible to allocate these doorstops to a particular area or factory, as most English glassworks made these items, very little value was attached to them, and the factories hardly ever kept records. There seems to be little point in researching a subject that has seen most of the producers no longer in business or swallowed up by larger firms. Every old glassworker I have spoken to has said, "yes, we made doorstops."

Paperweight and Miniature Paperweight, Nineteenth Century, Maker Unknown. ***Author's Collection.***

Left: Many paperweights made from green glass have these clay tablets inserted. They are usually crudely made with a variety of subjects. This paperweight has a hand offering a bunch of flowers, perhaps as a token of affection to a loved one. The weight is 3.4" high and 2.75" in diameter. The value is around $150-175. The base is unground with the pontil showing.

Right: This paperweight is a miniature, made from green glass with a foil flower set in a vase, and the first I have seen or heard of. It may have been made by the Kilner glass-house, but is not signed. The height is 2.4" and the diameter 1.7". This is a rare find but not of great value. A price of around $150 would be fair.

Paperweight with Thistles and Leaves, Nineteenth Century, Maker Unknown. Height 3.1". Dia. 2.75". $150-200. ***Courtesy of Anne Anderson.***

The thistle motif is very well constructed and must have taken quite some time to make. This leads me to believe that this was a production piece, probably made in some quantity and sold to the stationers and news agents of the time. The motif was cast in a mould, with a material that had the same or higher expansion rate as the glass, to prevent cracks and flaws appearing.

Paperweight with Small Standing Boy, Nineteenth Century, Maker Unknown. Height 3". Dia. 2.75". $150-200. ***Courtesy of Anne Anderson.***

A small boy floating in the centre of the weight with facial features that can just be seen.

Paperweight with Small Child Standing Waist Deep in Water, Nineteenth Century, Maker Unknown. Height 3.25". Dia. 2.25". $200-250. ***Courtesy of Mr. Skidmore's Collection.***

The tablet is made from a light colored clay material. The clay has given off oxygen in the heating process and has covered the figure with small bubbles. The little girl has wavy hair and appears to be standing in water as her legs are not visible. The weight is footed and in remarkably good condition, perhaps a treasured memento of someone's grandchild.

Inkwell with Marble Stopper, Late Nineteenth or Early Twentieth Century. Height 3.25". Dia. 2.75". $50-75. *Courtesy of Anne Anderson.*

This could be an office or school inkwell used by nearly everyone in the late nineteenth and early twentieth centuries. Again, because they were so common at the time, not many have survived in one piece and they are now quite rare.

Inkwell, Pale Green Glass with Bubbles. Height 5". $150-175. *Courtesy of Anne Anderson.*

Inkwells were a favorite of the many glasshouses, as they were reasonably easy to make and a popular buy with the public. They must have been produced by the millions in various shapes and forms. Because they were produced in such volume, very little value was attached, hence they became throwaway items. They are now quite rare and much appreciated by the antiques collector. To find one in good condition is an added bonus. This one with the original stopper is very decorative; it features sparkling glass with a hint of green and a few bubbles to decorate.

Inkwell with Stopper, Late Nineteenth or Early Twentieth Century. Height 2.5". Dia. 2.75". *Courtesy of Anne Anderson.*

An inkwell with a marble type stopper, clear pale green glass free from striations and bubbles. In excellent condition, $100-125.

Inkwell with Marble Stopper. Height 3.6". Dia. 3.3". $40-50. ***Author's Collection.***

The shapes and sizes of these inkwells are much the same whichever factory made them, but it would have been nice for the maker to sign them.

Inkwell, Nineteenth/Twentieth Century. Height 3.5". Dia. 3.75". $30-40. ***Authors Collection.***

This one has a very broad base and would be ideal for holding ink. A mass produced item for everyday use.

Doorstop with Prime Minister Gladstone (1809-89). Height 4.5". Dia. 2.9". $350-500. ***Courtesy of Mr. & Mrs. Richard Giles.***

A good portrait of the English Prime Minister Gladstone, who was in office four times between 1868 and 1894.

Doorstop with the Greek Goddess of Agriculture, Ceres. Height 4.5". Dia. 3". $350-500. ***Courtesy of Mr. & Mrs. Richard Giles.***

The Greek Goddess of food and plenty, Ceres, is seen carrying a basket of goods on her head.

Doorstop with Officer's Head Made from Clay Pipe. Height 3.5". Dia. 2.5". $250-400. ***Courtesy of Mr. & Mrs. Richard Giles.***

This inclusion of a clay pipe demonstrates the Apsley Pellatt method of including any material into glass that has a higher fusion point than the glass encasing it. The hole for the tobacco can be seen from above.

Doorstop with Trailed Glass. Height 4.5". Dia. 5". $300-350. ***Courtesy of Dr. Geoffrey Dutton.***

This is a rare doorstop, being one of the very few that contains another colored glass. The white trails of glass were pulled over the glass using a steel pin or comb, and then covered with more glass. In excellent condition, despite still being used as a doorstop.

Chapter Seven

H.G. Richardson Ltd.

Stourbridge, England

The Richardson family have been making glass in the Stourbridge area since the early nineteenth century. Glassmaking was brought to the area by a group of Huguenot workers in the late sixteenth century. They chose the area because of its proximity to the raw materials needed in glassmaking, mainly sand, fireclay, and coal for the furnaces. Initially, simple bottles and window glass were produced, but over the next two hundred years the trade developed into better quality and finer decorative pieces.

The Redhouse glassmaking cone was built around 1790 by Richard Bradley, a local industrialist. It was built on the side of the canal in the village of Wordsley, for the easy transportation of the raw materials. The funnel shape of the cone was designed to increase the draught of air through the building. The Redhouse cone is eighty-eight feet tall and fifty-nine feet in diameter. The glasshouse has changed hands many times since it was built, being owned by the Richardson family in the late nineteenth and early twentieth centuries.

The Richardson business was taken over by the Stuart Crystal Company in the 1920s. At the present time, this company is one of the world's largest producers of fine crystal tableware.

The Redhouse cone is now a museum and visitor centre, open to the public with a retail glass sales shop as well as a repair shop that undertakes paperweight restoration on site. Trips into the factory can also be made by prior arrangement. The rest of the site houses a café and glassworking shop, and the site is to be further developed to show such activities as cutting, engraving, and etching. It was at the Redhouse cone that the first reproduction of the famous Portland Vase was made by Richardson; the blank was then sent to the Brierley Hill Glassworks, where it was cut and engraved by John Northwood.

The shape of the half magnum paperweight shown on page 86 is a key factor to identifying paperweights and inkwells from Richardson, as it is a perfect match to drawings in the Richardson design books held in the Birmingham Art Gallery, England. One page of these design books shows a paperweight with the words "W. Smart Weights 12-12" and beneath this inscription, "Inks & Stoppers Ric." This could refer to the glassworks of W. Smart Ltd., who were a major glassworks in the area.. It may be that paperweights were being made for them as gifts or promotional aids, or possibly that the paperweights could have been contracted out for Smarts to make, although it would seem unlikely that Smarts, as the biggest glass producer in the area, would make such a small batch of paperweights and inkwells themselves. The Smarts glassworks were a major producer of sheet and industrial glass from early Victorian times and it would make commercial sense to contract out small orders that proved to be uneconomical, or for products that they were not used to producing.It would seem logical that as the drawings are in the Richardson pattern books, the paperweights and inkwells were made by the company themselves. The illustrated paperweight in the design book shows a magnum without any sizes quoted. A magnum in most paperweight circles is 3.5 inches or more; the one shown here is 3.8 inches in diameter. The drawing states that the weight of this magnum paperweight should be 2.75 pounds; on weighing this half of a paperweight, it shows almost exactly 1.35 pounds. The drawing shows a four row concentric with an inverted foot. This half is six rows with an inverted foot, but the paperweight in the other Richardson illustration shows a square cut, footed paperweight. The half paperweight here has a hollow ground-out base, with the set-up of canes floating almost halfway into the glass dome. The barely discernible writing on the pattern books describes the colors to be used, starting from the centre as follows:

Centre White Ruby (outside)?
Amber White (outside)?
Blue White (outside)?
Pale Amber (White outside)?
White Blue Green (White outside)?

The half paperweight shows some very similar color combinations, not the least of which is a rarely seen amber colored cane. From the centre the colors are:

Centre Amber, Ruby outside
Blue, White outside
Amber, White outside
Amber, Ruby outside
Blue White, White outside
White

The outside cane is an all white quatrefoil, and this cane can be found in other weights that, up until now, have had an unidentified maker. The precision with which the canes are set is another factor in this group of paperweights and inkwells. Of the many hundreds of old English pieces I have seen, I have never seen anything to compare with the preciseness of the cane size and placement in these Richardson weights.

Richardson Inkwell Without Stopper, c. 1915. Height 4". Dia. 3.7". $300-400. ***Author's Collection.***

An inkwell with the same precise structure and cane set-up as with other examples. The outside row of all white quatrefoil canes are the same as in the half a paperweight shown on page 86. The inkwell has six precisely set rows around a large central star cane, and sits on an inverted rim.

The Redhouse Glass Cone, Stourbridge, c. 1902.

The site still looks the same today; little has changed in the last ninety-five years.

Base of Richardson Inkwell.

The base shows the canes drawn only to the edge of the cane set-up. Because the canes were cut to the exact length required there are no uneven rod ends to be seen. This makes for an attractive base finish and distinguishes this glassworks from many of the other makers of the period. Unlike the half paperweight, this inkwell has a rough pontil.

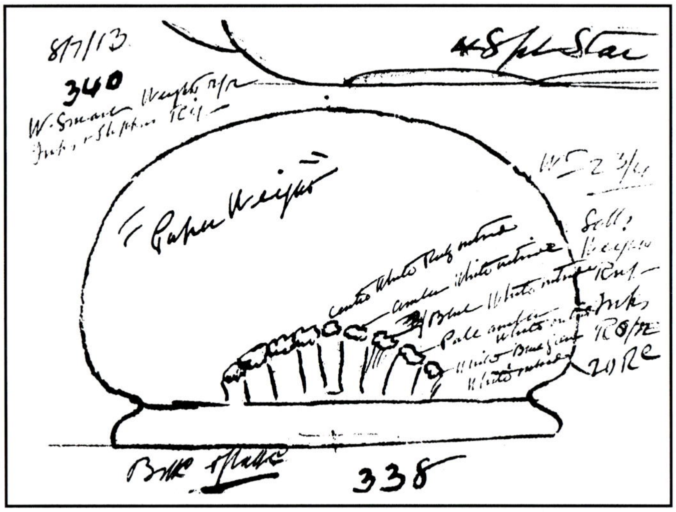

Design for a magnum paperweight by H.G. Richardson & Sons, dated 1913.

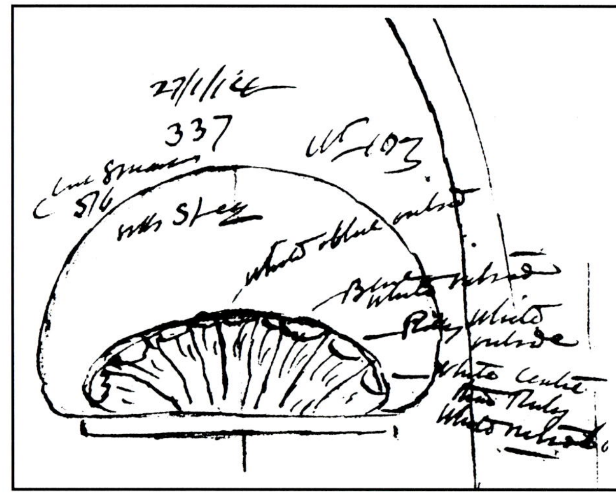

Design for a paperweight by H.G. Richardson & Sons, dated 1914.

H.G. Richardson Six Row Concentric Magnum, c. 1913. Height 2.6". Dia. 3.8". *Author's Collection.*

There is little or no value to this beautiful magnum paperweight, as it is only one half of the original. At some point in the past, it must have been dropped on a hard surface to have shattered into two pieces. However, the bit that remains has a value beyond money as it opens the door to identifying paperweights and inkwells from the Richardson Glassworks.

Profile of Richardson Paperweight. Height 2.6".

The profile of this magnum has a crown that is almost flat before falling steeply down to the base. Also, the cane set-up is lying flatly near the centre of the paperweight.

Base of Richardson Paperweight. Dia. 3.8".

The base is concave with a very narrow basal rim. The pontil has been ground out and polished, leaving a smooth and clear base that shows the cane ends, which are so precisely cut and placed as to be a mirror image of the paperweight crown. This paperweight was a quality piece from the glassmakers of Stourbridge, an area rich in the artistry and skills of glass making.

H.G. Richardson Five Row Concentric, c. 1915. Height 2.7". Dia. 3.5". (Part of a Three Piece Set) $750-850 for Individual Paperweight. ***Author's Collection.***

A very fine example of a Richardson paperweight. The canes are set precisely around a simple red and white hollow cog cane. This central cane rather lets the weight down in terms of interest. The weight could have been so much better if any of the other canes in the weight had been used instead, either singly or as a group. But the set-up of canes is quite special, as the sizes have been matched and set together perfectly. The outside row of white quatrefoil canes are the same as in the previous Richardson examples.

Base of Five Row Richardson Paperweight.

Again the base shows the precision and trouble that Richardson took with the finishing off of a paperweight. The cane ends are cut to the right lengths and not drawn beneath the base. The pontil has been left unground. The base is slightly concave, so that the rough pontil would not touch any surface it was placed upon. The reason that the factory did not grind out the pontil on all the weights they made, when they went to so much trouble to get the canes right, mystifies me. The base has a squarely cut foot.

Set of Richardson Paperweights and Inkwell, c. 1915. $2500-3000. ***Author's Collection.***

A matching set of paperweights and inkwell.

H.G. Richardson Six Row Concentric Paperweight, c. 1915. Height 2.5". Dia. 4". $500-600. ***Courtesy of Terry and Hilary Johnson.***

A good example of the precise cane set-up from Richardson. The six rows are centred on a larger red, white, and blue star cane. The profile is the same as the previous examples attributed to the Richardson Glassworks.

Base of Richardson Paperweight.

The base shows an inverted foot, with the canes drawn down to the edges only. The rough pontil is broken flush with the concave base, and does not protrude.

Richardson Five Row Footed Inkwell, c. 1915. Height 7". Dia. 4.25". $1000-1250. *Author's Collection.*

This inkwell has the same precisely set canes, all cut to the correct lengths, as the other paperweights and inkwells that I have attributed to the Richardson Glassworks. These features are not found in any other English millefiori paperweight or related pieces, except Whitefriars, which I will review in another chapter. Although the shape of this inkwell does not conform to the shape in the Richardson pattern book, i.e. this stopper has a knob on the stem and the sides of the inkwell rise more steeply. I feel that the well-made canes and set-up look more like Richardson than any other English maker. When the glassworkers were producing paperweights and inkwells they must have had some degree of artistic license to vary shapes and sizes, unless they were involved on a production run, when they would have used all their skill to try and produce items of a uniform size and shape.

Base of Richardson Inkwell.

The base shows a slight concavity and an unground pontil mark. The cane ends are precisely cut to length and are set on a low cushion quite close to the bottom of the inkwell. The cushion rises about a third of the way into the dome. The inkwell sits on an inverted foot. A handwritten label by the dealer who sold this inkwell attributed the piece to Whitefriars. This was a reasonable assumption since this was a typically English style of cane set-up. Most other English pieces of similar quality and style were also named as Whitefriars because we were not aware until quite recently of the Richardson, Arculus, and Walsh-Walsh glassworks' production of paperweights and inkwells. The label shows a price of 20 shillings, which was the equivalent of £1 Sterling or $3 US Dollars.

Five Row Concentric. Height 2.5". Dia. 3.4". $450-550. ***Courtesy of Mr. and Mrs. Richard Giles.***

Another nice example of precisely set canes which seems to be the hallmark of these high domed, footed paperweights attributed to Richardson. The quality of these weights is so much better than the weights that were made around the early part of the twentieth century by Arculus, Walsh-Walsh, and some other unknown makers.

Profile of Five Row Concentric.

The profile shows the deeply inverted foot and the outer row of canes drawn down to the centre of the base. The low cushion reaches out to the edge of the weight to the steep sides.

Richardson Four Row Concentric Inkwell. Height 5.5". Dia. 2.8". $650-750. ***Private Collection.***

This inkwell has the same meticulous cane set-up as previous examples of paperweights and inkwells from Richardson. All the canes are cut to the same exact lengths and set low in the base of the piece. The base has a rough pontil and is footed. The four rows of canes are centred on a large blue and white cog cane. The stopper is equally as well made, and matches the set-up in the base.

Richardson Six Row Concentric Inkwell. Height 6". $600-700. ***Courtesy of "The Sweetbriar Gallery," Helsby, England.***

Another inkwell, slightly taller and narrower than the previous example, but with the same beautifully constructed cane set up, especially difficult with six rows to contend with. The stopper shows the same amount of attention to detail as the base.

Richardson Faceted Magnum Five Row Concentric. Height 3". Dia. 3.8". $500-600. ***Author's Collection.***

Seven and one facets and an inverted foot complement this lovely magnum from the Richardson Glassworks. The canes sit low down in the bottom of the weight, with two rows of matching canes as found in the half weight shown earlier. The skills in cane sizing and dexterity demonstrated by the cane setters are quite remarkable. The use of small canes is similar to the modern styles of Baccarat and Saint Louis. I have visited both these French factories only recently, and have watched the men and women setting up these canes into ring moulds, a long and painstaking job but rewarding when completed.

Five Row Concentric. Height 2.75". Dia. 3.75". $900-1000 (for pair). ***Courtesy of Dr. Geoffrey Dutton.***

One of a pair of very precise paperweights that are in pristine condition. The well-matched canes are set around a thick white pastry mould cane, which is on the large side and looks quite clumsy against the rest of the finely made, matched canes. This is a notable feature with many English weights. The central cane should be the most special cane in the whole paperweight, but in most cases it isn't.

Chapter Eight

Arculus

Broad Street, Birmingham, England

Alfred Arculus and Joseph Warry were employed as accounts clerks at the firm of R.W. Winfield, Brassfounders, 42/45, Broad Street, Birmingham. From 1864 the firm produced silver and electroplated wares. Flint glass was produced as a sideline to the main business. The two men took over the firm in 1875 as equal partners and moved the business to 295, Broad Street, Birmingham. The company was renamed Alfred Arculus & Co., and in 1876 the company was listed in *Kellys Trades Directory* for the first time. Their principal activities were the manufacturing of flint glass, chandeliers, and glass fittings, having apparently dropped the brass foundry business. The same year the business was started, Alfred Arculus died; following his death his two sons Edward and Noel were given shares in the business. They joined the firm under the guidance of Alfred's partner, Joseph Warry. Edward Arculus died in 1907 and Noel Arculus died in 1911. After their deaths the aging Joseph Warry invited Noel's two sons, Thomas and Noel junior, to join the business, and made each of them head of a department. Thomas took charge of the glasshouse and lighting department and Noel ran the reproduction of antiques, crystal, and cutting shop.

In 1922 the firm was bought out by T.J. Hands & Son, but carried on with the name Arculus, with no apparent change to the business. T.J. Hands also had a glassworks at 86, Lodge Road, Birmingham. In the 1924 April edition of *The Pottery Gazette & Trade Review* a statement about the firm was written as follows: "Arculus & Co. revels in producing things difficult to obtain elsewhere, and have always been in the vanguard of the lighting glass trade. The backbone of the business are the specialty lines, richly cut, distinctive antique reproductions of handmade salad bowls, candlesticks, goblets, water jugs, celery vases, toilet sets etc. etc."

In 1931 the Arculus name and factory in Broad Street was bought out by John Walsh Walsh Ltd. The business remained, with little or no changes to production at this factory until it was destroyed by a German landmine in 1941. At the present time the site is occupied by the Hyatt Hotel, which sits on the edge of the canal that was once the main route for the raw materials used by the glassmakers of Arculus and Walsh. In 1932 Thomas and Noel Arculus left the employment of Walsh-Walsh, either as part of the buy-out deal, or to do their own thing. *Kellys*, the Birmingham trades directory, shows that the two brothers (who were the best of friends and "inseparable" according to Arculus family members who remember them) are listed as Glass Manufacturers, 61 Livery Street, Birmingham. The brothers continued to make glass until 1941, when the business was terminated with some acrimony. It is not known as yet what type of glass they produced, but it would be reasonable to assume paperweights and inkwells were a probable product, given the brothers' history in the reproduction of antiques. The career of the brothers after this period is not certain, although Noel's son remembers his father working as a company salesman.

Thanks to a chance encounter with a member of the Arculus family at the Broadfield House Museum, Kingswinford, England, the museum's glass Curator, Roger Dodsworth, discovered that the Arculus family still had objects, including paperweights, that were definitely made in the 1920-30s, and which contained 1848 date canes. Roger arranged to see and photograph the items for an article that subsequently appeared in the *1995 Paperweight Collector's Association Annual Bulletin*. The article was entitled "1848 & All That" and went on to show that paperweights and inkwells with 1848 canes were in fact made for the antiques trade in the 1920s and '30s. With these authentic pieces from the Arculus family, and canes given to the museum by the son of a former worker at the Walsh-Walsh factory, it is now possible to identify Arculus and Walsh-Walsh weights that have been attributed to the wrong factories, usually Whitefriars.

I have tried to contact as many of the remaining Arculus family that have millefiori objects still in their possession, and was pleasantly surprised to find that two others had objects made by the Arculus glasshouse in addition to the objects discovered by Roger

Dodsworth. The first was a massive, five-sided doorstop, similar to the doorstop shown in the P.C.A. bulletin, and another family member had a few canes and a superb selection of general glasswares and vases made by the Arculus firm. In a letter to an Arculus family member who is researching his family tree, the grandson of the joint founder of the business (also named Joseph Warry) says that he worked alongside Thomas and Noel junior just before and after the 1914-18 war. He started work for Arculus in 1913 and it was his job to type out envelopes and invoices to the customers to whom they sold the reproduction glass. These customers included Page & Newton and Minshull. The maiden name of Alfred Arculus' wife was Minshull, and another Arculus family member also ran a hardware shop in Birmingham called "Minshull Arculus Hardware" Hardware Merchants, 89, Leopold Street. The hardware retailers in England could also sell glass, ceramics, and many other non-related hardware items. Could this Minshull have been one of the outlets for the reproduction items made by the family glasshouse? When Alfred Arculus died, his wife retained his share interest in the Arculus business. In the 1881 census, she describes herself as Mary Arculus, aged fifty-six, glass and chandelier manufacturer, employing seventy-one men, eighteen boys, and six women.

Joseph Warry (1845-1921). Joint founder of Alfred Arculus & Co.

Alfred Arculus (1824-1875). Joint founder of Alfred Arculus & Co.

Robert Noel Arculus (1887-1954). He was nicknamed "Noely" and ran the reproduction of antiques department at the Arculus Glassworks.

Mary Arculus (nee Minshull), 1824-1898.

Frederick Minshull Arculus (1896-1981). Ran Minshull Arculus Hardware Merchants, at 89 Leopold Street, Birmingham, between 1948 and 1961.

Alfred Noel Arculus, born 1911.

Alfred Noel Arculus is the son of Robert Noel Arculus, who ran the reproduction of antiques department at the Arculus Glassworks, Birmingham, from 1911 to 1931. At a meeting with Alfred, held at his home near Redditch on the outskirts of Birmingham, I was pleased to talk to a man who had earned his pocket money helping to set up the millefiori canes in cast iron ring moulds for use at the Arculus Glassworks. When I first mentioned that I was researching a book on Old English Paperweights, his face lit up. "Did you find any with date canes in?" he asked. "Yes," I replied, "many paperweights and inkwells have an 1848 date cane in the outer rows." "I put those dates in," said Alfred. He went on to explain how his father would bring the already cut to length canes home for him to set up after school and weekends. He would set the canes into concentric rings or close packs in patterns and colors decided by himself. The set-ups would then be returned to the factory for use in paperweights, inkwells, candlesticks, shot glasses, and many other items. He well remembers watching the set-ups he had made being used by the glassmakers on his numerous visits to the Glassworks. Alfred went on to describe how his Auntie Dorothy (Dorothy Ellen Arculus, 1892-1987) was the main person responsible for the setting up of the moulds, and how she had shown him how to antique the bases; she slid the paperweights and other items backwards and forwards on a steel plate, on a sand and dirt bed, but not always in the same direction. She said, "vary the direction you move the pieces, to make the scratches look authentic." Alfred was only a ten or eleven-year-old boy at the time in question, and has a good memory. However, I had taken along several dated paperweights which he recognized as the same style and cane set-ups as he had made, but he could not say definitely that they were set up by himself or Dorothy. He did, however, recognize the date canes, and said that 1848 was the only date used but did not know the reason for that date only. Alfred also had in his possession several lengths of millefiori cane of a basic cog design. He did not know if Arculus made their own canes or if they were bought in. He could not recall ever having seen silhouette canes of rabbits, horses or any head silhouettes. He was also the proud owner of a substantial amount of the Arculus Glassworks better-made vases and wineglasses, passed onto him by his father. His last recollection of the Arculus factory was a visit he and his father had taken to see the factory in Broad Street, Birmingham, after the German landmine had completely destroyed it. The site now has a hotel built on it.

Arculus Glassworks, Broad Street, Birmingham. c. 1914. ***Courtesy of Joseph Warry, born 1896.***

The Glassworks were conveniently situated on the canal side for easy access of bulk deliveries of sand and fuels. This drawing was done from memory by the original descendant of Joseph Warry.

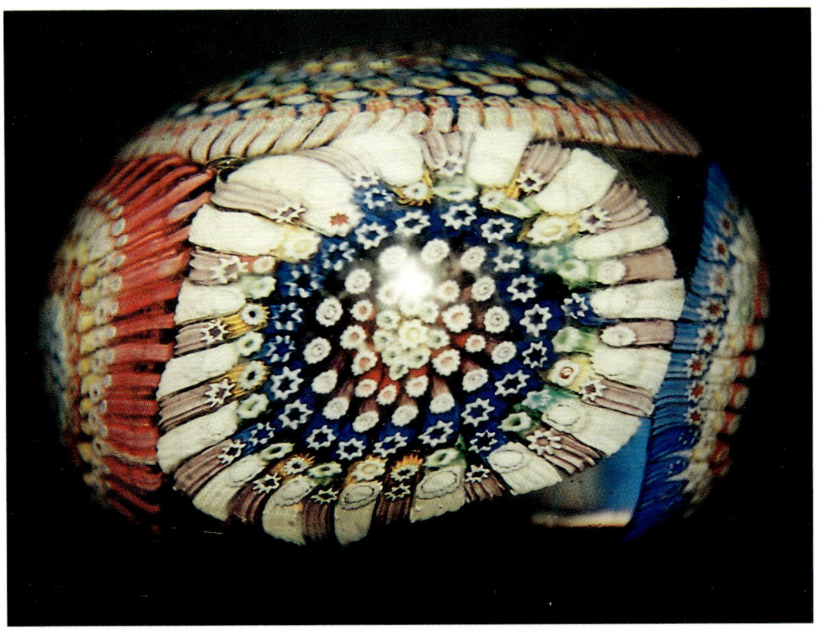

Arculus Doorstop, c. 1920. Height 3.6". Dia. 5.8". $3000. ***Courtesy of Thomas Guy Arculus.***

This enormous doorstop is almost the same as the doorstop featured in the 1995 P.C.A. article on Arculus. This piece can be used to reference Arculus paperweights and millefiori objects. I have shown all four sides and the base so all the canes can be seen, including the rough pontil. The canes can be in soft or hard colors, with the majority being cogs, stars, and tubes.

Base of Doorstop.

Looking inside the base, the cane ends can be seen cut, or tapered, by heat, in varying untidy lengths between 0.25" and 0.5". The component parts of this doorstop are the same as used for paperweight manufacture, and show a low dome with a large diameter in comparison. The large pontil can still be seen and was not removed by grinding. The base shows a shallow concavity created before the pontil was snapped off. The piece sits on a wide basal ring for stability.

Side of Doorstop.

A seven row concentric in mainly blue cogs and star canes. Concentrics were the mainstay of Arculus production, with very few close packs made.

Side of Doorstop.

This view shows a close pack arrangement of canes, but using only cogs, tubes, and stars in various colors including lilac and pale green.

Side of Doorstop.

Seven rows of canes, mainly cogs and stars, but one row of blue and white canes with what has been described as a window cane. This cane has white parts squeezed at the waist to form sometimes two and sometimes four sections. Unfortunately, this cane can be seen also in Walsh-Walsh paperweights and inkwells, to further confuse the collector of English weights. The precise year of manufacture is unknown, along with all the following paperweights and other millefiori objects, but remember that Walsh-Walsh bought the Arculus Glassworks and presumably ran their own factory alongside the Arculus business until Arculus was bombed out in 1941. The interchanging of canes was inevitable if this is the case.

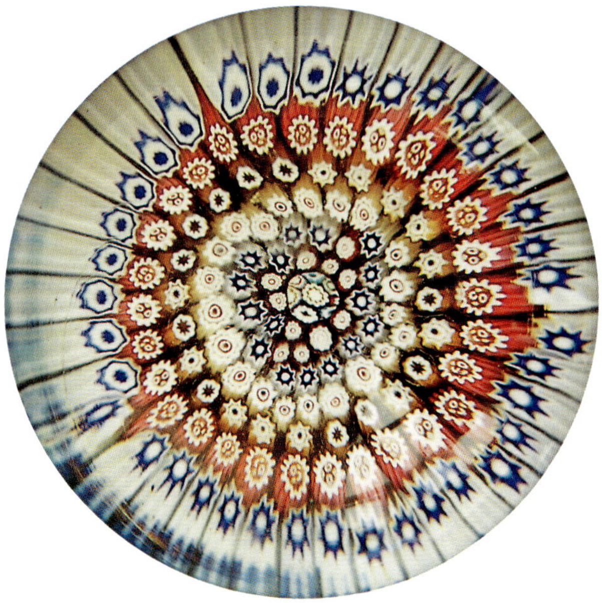

Arculus Six Row Magnum Concentric, c, 1920, Dia. 3.75". $400-500.
Author's Collection.

An important paperweight, for identification purposes, as the unusual pink cane in the second row from the outside is identical to a cane in the Arculus family piece (Fig. 6 in the P.C.A. "1848 and all That" article), but the pink and white row of canes near the centre matches exactly a cane shown in the same article with one of the Walsh-Walsh canes given to the Broadfield House Museum by the son of a former worker at the Walsh glassworks. This clearly demonstrates the near impossibility of dating accurately when a piece was made by either of these factories. The movement of canes and workers between the Arculus/Hands Glassworks and the Walsh-Walsh Glassworks in the 1920s and '30s is almost certainly the reason for the appearance of Walsh and Arculus canes in the same weight. The pink and white cog in the second row has, in the centre, two circles and two broken pieces of a circle, and is easily identifiable with the Arculus family piece. The six rows are loosely packed together with several canes slipping to distort the set-up. The central cane is a combination of simple cog canes encased to make a single complex cane. Arculus made no serious attempt at creating beautiful or imaginative complex canes like Bacchus or the French paperweight makers; the canes were dipped into various different colored glass for variety.

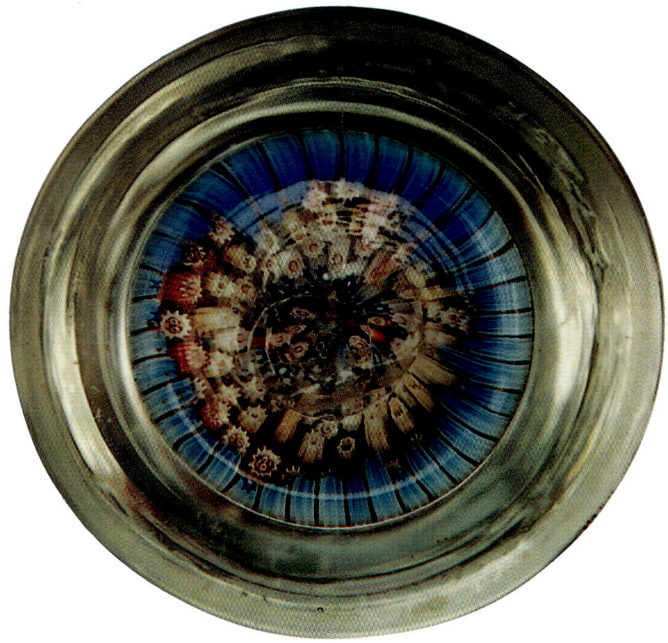

Base of Six Row Magnum Concentric.

The base shows the relatively small size of the cane set-up to the size of the glass encasing them. The canes have been picked up by the final gather of glass by pressing the soft glass onto the canes. This method leaves a ridge between the two halves that can be felt with the tips of the fingers and is quite distinctive. Many English paperweights show this ridge, and it was thought that the ridge was the main identifying feature of Whitefriars. Whitefriars Glass were producing paperweights by this method from the early 1950s to 1981 when the factory was closed. The pontil mark has been left unground, and this unground pontil is a feature of all the Arculus family items. The canes are drawn down and under the base and left with uneven ends, varying from 0.25" to 0.75".

Profile of Six Row Magnum Concentric. Height 2.1".

The profile of this weight shows a steep sided dome with the top almost flat. The cushion of canes are set low in the base of the weight. From every angle the canes seem to start right on the edge of the weight, but in fact are nearly one inch from the sides, highlighting the dramatic effect of the glass' magnifying properties on the small canes

Arculus Five Row Magnum Concentric, c. 1920. Height 2.1". Dia. 3.75". $400-500. *Author's Collection.*

This paperweight can also be reliably used for identification purposes. It is identical in height diameter and cane construction to the Arculus family paperweights. This weight shows a good central feature cane. This cane reoccurs as the outside row and the inside row. The colors are blended together with a little thought and the set-up is nicely done, making this paperweight a good example from the Arculus factory. It would seem that not all millefiori items were sold to the antiques trade by Arculus, as this would have flooded the market. It must have been the dated 1848 examples only. The undated pieces were probably sold to wholesalers and merchants for sale everywhere. The profile and base are identical to the previous paperweight.

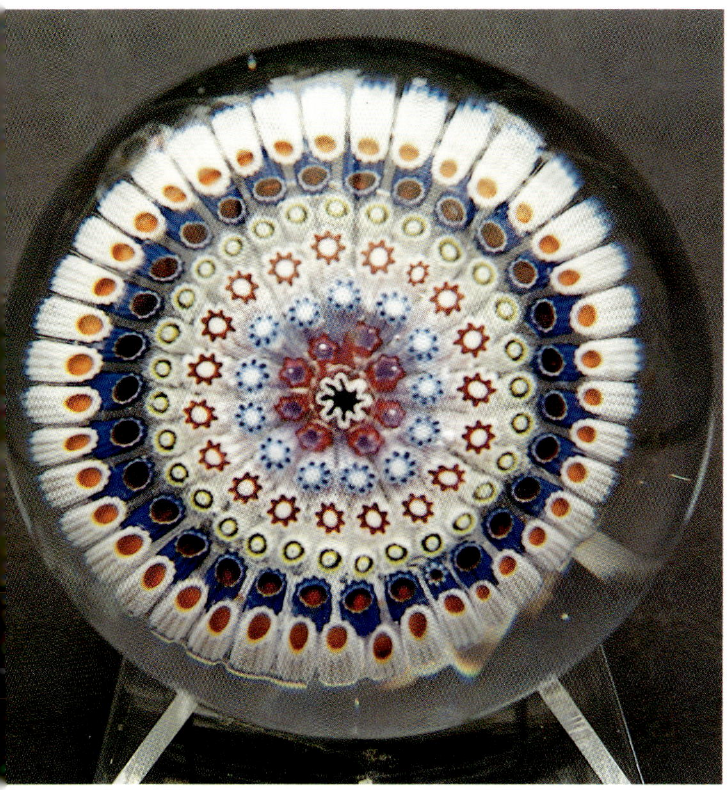

Arculus Six Row Concentric, c. 1920. Height 2.2". Dia. 3.7". $400-500. *Courtesy of Mr. Skidmore's Collection.*

This paperweight has all the same features as the previous Arculus weights but this one has a foot on the base to make it different. Their are no hard and fast rules with English paperweight makers of the 1920s and '30s. Because there were no vast production runs of weights, the shapes, sizes, set-ups, and canes were left to the individual worker. As long as the general guidelines were adhered to, the individual weight was finished as the glassworker pleased. This would account for the odd paperweight that is slightly different from the rest but still has the majority of features to identify it as from the same factory.

Base of Six Row Concentric.

The base looks identical to the other Arculus paperweights with the exception of the foot that recesses the base by 0.3".

Arculus Shot Glasses, c. 1920. Height 1.5". Base Dia. 1". $75-100 per piece. ***Author's Collection.***

A selection of shot or tot glasses, the same as one held by the Arculus family of which a photograph is unobtainable for publication. I have seen the original photograph and can verify these glasses are identical to the glass held by the family. A ridge can be felt where the small set-up of canes was picked up. Over the last forty or fifty years these small glasses have been described as Saint Louis and Whitefriars, but in my discussion with Alfred Noel Arculus (born 1911) he recalled that such glasses were made by his father at the Arculus works. The Whitefriars shot glass is much taller, and was made between 1950 and 1980. Saint Louis also made many items with millefiori included in the bases, such as candlesticks, vases, and the like, which look very similar to these Arculus items. The main distinguishing feature between these two glass-houses is the usually untidy cane set-ups from Arculus, with Saint Louis items being extremely precise in the cane set-up process.

Bases of Shot Glasses.

The canes are drawn to the centres of the glasses to leave a neat finish. A small ridge where the set-up of canes joins the sides of the glass can be felt with the fingertips.

Close-up of Shot Glass.

Close-up of Shot Glass.

Close-up of Shot Glass.

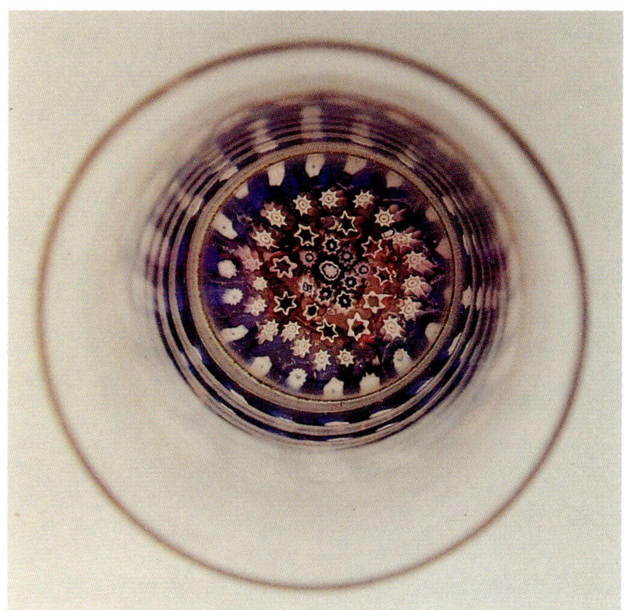

Close-up of Shot Glass.

Arculus Miniature Paperweight, c. 1920. Height 1.1". Dia. 2.5". $250-300. *Author's Collection.*

A rare Arculus miniature of the same size and shape as one held by the Arculus family. Unfortunately, no photographs can be obtained of the family-owned miniature for publication. However, I have seen a photograph of it and can say that this piece is identical.

Base of Miniature.

The base shows the same construction as a full-size paperweight, including the well-defined ridge between the two gathers of glass. The pontil has been left unground.

Profile Of Miniature Paperweight.

The profile shows the same low dome as with some of the Arculus full-size paperweights.

Arculus Six Row Concentric, c. 1920. Height 1.5". Dia. 3.25". $400-500. *Author's Collection.*

A six row, low domed concentric, with varied canes set around a large white and blue cog cane. This paperweight is exactly the same size as the Arculus family piece illustrated in the P.C.A. bulletin. The canes on the second row from the edge look like a hollow tube with a red candle and white wick showing. Trefoil canes are found in the second row from the centre. The profile shows the dome falling smoothly to the base.

Base of Arculus Low Domed Paperweight.

The base shows the cane ends neatly finished and cut uniformly to length. The pontil has been removed by hollow grinding. This gives the paperweight the look and feel of a discus or frisbee. This weight could have been made during the ownership of T.J. Hands or Walsh-Walsh. Although it has the same dimensions as Arculus weights, it is a definite improvement on the former.

Arculus Six Row Concentric, c. 1920. Height 1.5". Dia. 3.25". $400-500. *Author's Collection.*

This paperweight is identical in size and construction to the previous weight. The canes are very similar to canes also found in Walsh-Walsh paperweights and the attribution to a single glass-works at a specific date is almost impossible.

Base of Arculus Low Domed Paperweight.

On this base, the cane ends are drawn under but not as tidily as in the former weight. The distinctive ridge between the gathers of glass has caused confusion with the Whitefriars Glassworks, as this method of picking up the cane set-up was considered their trademark.

Profile of Arculus Low Domed Paperweight.

The profile shows the low and steep sides on this type of paperweight from Arculus.

Arculus "1848" Dated, Low Domed Seven Row Concentric. Height 1.5". Dia. 3.75". $600-700. ***Courtesy of The Stone Gallery, Burford, England.***

This paperweight has the same date canes as the Arculus family-owned pieces. The blue letters on opal white can be seen in the second row from the edge. The seven rows of canes make this weight a little different, as does the sugar candy coloring of the outside row. The base has been hollow ground, quite deeply, to remove the pontil mark.

Arculus Eight Row Concentric, c. 1920. Height 1.5". Dia. 3.3". $700-800. ***Courtesy of Anne Anderson.***

An average sized paperweight that has an amazing eight rows of canes. The outside row has forty-two canes. Although the canes are simple cogs and stars, all centred on a small blue and white cog cane, the weight is still desirable for its rarity. There are not many weights to be seen with eight rows. The base is hollow ground with a ridge mark.

Magnum Chequer Weight. Height 2.5". Dia. 3.9". $300-400. ***Author's Collection.***

Chequer weights were extremely difficult to make because of the canes slipping when picking up the paperweight with the final coating of glass. The French glassmakers Clichy and Baccarat were the only successful glassworks to achieve this procedure. Chequer weights command prices in excess of $2500 because of the rarity and degree of difficulty in making a successful piece. In this weight, the paperweight maker has achieved a certain success, but has used canes of poor quality and variable lengths. If the canes had been cut to equal length the piece would have been that much better. This is quite a rare paperweight; I have only seen one other, which is featured later in this chapter. This other piece has the same untidy cane lengths which were are colored red. The canes in both weights are almost identical. The other weight was listed as nineteenth century, probably Whitefriars. My paperweight was bought in a Birmingham auction room in 1996, and has canes that can now be matched to canes in the pieces belonging to the Arculus family. The base has a slight concavity, with the pontil removed by grinding. The base has a layer of blue glass flashed up to the base of the canes. As Arculus were known to reproduce antiques for the collecting public, could this have been an attempt to copy the antique French Clichy chequers that have become so collectible and rare? This piece has a letter J cane on the outside edge. Arculus paperweights are normally left with ragged cane ends and rough pontils, Baccarat and Clichy always finished their bases with precision and a slight concavity as this piece has.

Six Row Concentric. Height 1.4". Dia. 2.75". $450-550. *Courtesy of Mr. & Mrs. Richard Giles.*

A well-presented paperweight from Arculus. The central blue and white encased cane is circled by six rows of simple cog canes. The low dome reaches down to the base which has a slight concavity and rough pontil mark. This paperweight would have been made around the early part of the twentieth century.

Re-Faceted, Close Packed Millefiori, Dated 1848. *Courtesy of Dr. Geoffrey Dutton.*

This is one of the rarer paperweights from Arculus. The close packs from this glassworks were used to make up the sides of the enormous doorstops as seen on previous pages. Unusually, the date canes are placed near to the centre, which would help to prevent slippage during the making process. The dates are normally found in the first or second row from the outside in concentrics. The weight is also faceted, which is a rarity for Arculus, as very few of their paperweight and inkwell production varied in style from their normal concentrics. More likely, this weight has suffered serious damage in the past and has been reground to remove the damage.

Arculus Chequer Paperweight, c. 1920. Height 1.9". Dia 3.3". $750-1000. *Courtesy of Bill Volkman.*

There are several known chequer weights the same as this piece, which was sold at auction and labeled as "Early Whitefriars." The correct attributions can now be made to the Arculus glasshouse. The weight bears all the features of this company's paperweights. Firstly, it is a copy of well-known chequer weights made by the Clichy glass house. The quality of this copy bares no resemblance to the complex and carefully arranged canes from Clichy. This weight has canes and latticinio rods all loosely arranged, which has resulted in slippage and distorted rods. Secondly, and most importantly, the individual segments of the complex canes in this weight can be matched to canes in the known Arculus family pieces. The construction and making of a chequer paperweight is one of the most difficult of processes, and credit must be given to Arculus for the attempt. If they had achieved a quality product, I'm sure we could have looked forward to dated 1848 pieces turning up as well.

Base of Arculus Chequer Paperweight.

Clichy made chequer weights on a bed of latticinio rods; in this weight the technique has been copied using only four or five large pieces against the many Clichy would use.

Arculus Paneled Paperweight, c. 1920. Height 1.9". Dia. 3.5". $750-1000. ***Courtesy of Bill Volkman.***

Untidy canes make up this paneled weight from Arculus, which again is a copy of an antique French paperweight. This is the first of this type of paperweight from Arculus I have ever seen, and may be unique; if not unique it is certainly very rare. The canes can be matched to known Arculus canes.

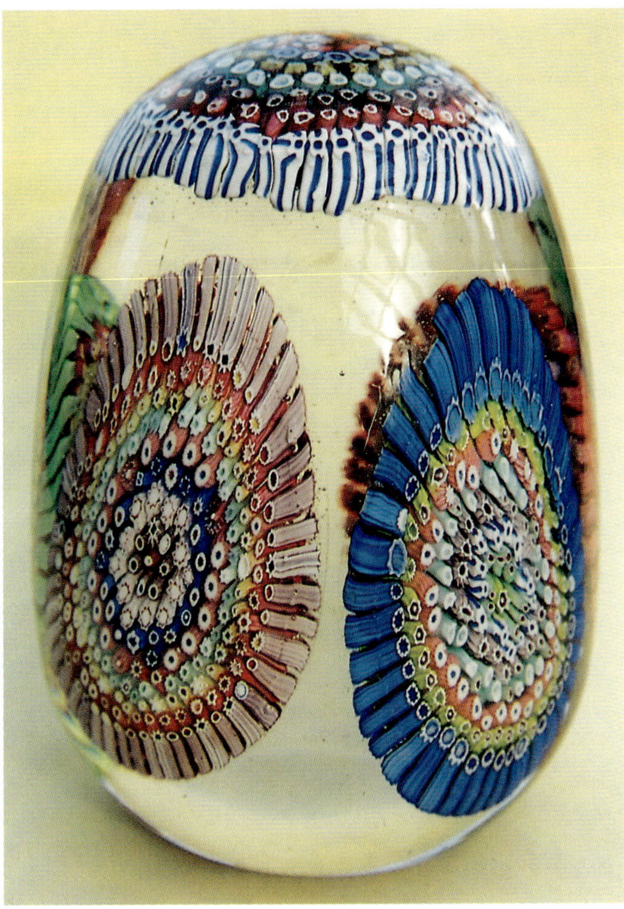

Table Ornament or Doorstop. Height 6". Dia. 4.5". $1500-1750. ***Courtesy of Terry and Hilary Johnson.***

Unlike the other known examples of these massive doorstops, this piece is a bullet shape, and in a very good condition. The base shows plenty of wear on the basal ring and has a rough pontil mark. The piece has four paperweights on the sides with one as a top feature. Typically, the canes are all set rather untidily in rows of many mis-matched canes. All the sides show concentric weights.

Close-up of Table Ornament or Doorstop.

This close-up of one of the sides shows figure-eight canes near the centre of the weight, and also the seven and six canes which were so popular in paperweights from the Arculus glassworks.

Chapter Nine

Walsh-Walsh

112, Lodge Road, Birmingham, England

The Walsh-Walsh glassworks was built in 1801 but not acquired by them until 1850. The period we are concerned with is the years between 1931 and 1951. It was during the period 1915-30 that paperweights began to be collected seriously by the general public. The rising prices for antique weights and the resulting publicity in collectors' journals and newspaper articles also brought weights to the attention of glassmakers, who had the necessary skills to reproduce these ingenious glass curiosities. The favourite date in these reproduction pieces was 1848; the reproducers probably chose that date because it coincided with the peak production from the French glasshouses of Baccarat, St. Louis, and Clichy, and was the date most frequently found in the genuine antiques, especially from Baccarat.

We know that the Arculus company was making paperweights and inkwells in the early 1920s with fake dates, and it is probable that Walsh-Walsh did so around the same time, or shortly afterwards. It has been established that Walsh made paperweights before 1928, thanks to a letter sent to the English newspaper *The Daily Express*. A Mr. Parkes wrote to the Express in 1977 referring to an article published by the newspaper on paperweights, and went on to describe how he made cane set-ups for Walsh-Walsh Co. Ltd in January 1928 as his first job with the company. He described in some detail how he inserted the 1848 date canes in the second row from the outside in blue letters on an opal ground. He also described how the millefiori paperweights and inkwells were "antiqued" by rubbing the bases with coarse sand ready to sell to the "Americans and other so called experts" as genuine antiques. Mr. Parkes stayed with the company until its close in 1951 due to the ill health of its single director. Mr. Parkes achieved the status of Works Manager, and I would consider his letter genuine. He went on to say that paperweights and other millefiori items were only a sideline for the company, as they were quality glass suppliers to the retail trade, supplying the likes of Aspreys, Mappin & Webb, and many other prestigious outlets.

The puzzling thing about this company is why, if they supplied such quality outlets, did they get involved in the faking of antique glassware and risk the reputation of the company? In 1931 John Walsh-Walsh took over the Arculus Glassworks in Broad Street, Birmingham, from the then owners T.J. Hands Ltd. Walsh-Walsh had their head office as Lodge Road, Birmingham, but also had a glassworks at 86 Cecil Street, Birmingham. It would be reasonable to assume that the glassworks in Broad Street, now owned by Walsh-Walsh, continued to produce paperweights and other millefiori objects until it was destroyed in 1941 by a German landmine, and that they continued to produce millefiori pieces from their other premises in Birmingham until they closed in 1951.

Walsh-Walsh Canes, c. 1930. ***Courtesy of Broadfield House Glass Museum, Kingswinford, England.***

These canes were donated to the Broadfield House Glass Museum, Kingswinford, England by William Philip Kirkham, born 1924. His father had been an employee at the Walsh-Walsh glassworks from 1914 until the works closed in 1951. Mr. Kirkham senior had been employed to set up the millefiori canes into moulds ready for encasing with glass and making into inkwells and paperweights. Among these canes are numbers and animals, including rabbits and horses.

Selection of Canes by John Walsh-Walsh, c. 1930. ***Courtesy of The Broadfield House Glass Museum, Kingswinford, England.***

Anonymous Canes, Possibly Walsh-Walsh or Arculus. ***Courtesy of The Broadfield House Glass Museum, Kingswinford, England.***

This selection of canes bought at auction in 1992 by the Broadfield House Glass Museum are of a mainly simple construction, with many of the individual canes appearing in paperweights and inkwells attributed to Arculus and Walsh-Walsh. The canes have the same coloring and structure of many of the canes given by Mr. Kirkham to the Glass Museum, and possibly originated from the same source.

Anonymous Canes, Possibly Walsh-Walsh or Arculus. ***Courtesy of Broadfied House Glass Museum.***

A selection of canes given to the Glass Museum containing very similar canes in structure and coloring, probably from the same source as the previous canes. The bottom row in this photograph has a rabbit and the letter B.

Walsh-Walsh, Dated 1848 Concentric Paperweight, c. 1930. Dia. 3.2". $700-900. *Private Collection.*

A fine, six row concentric, nicely arranged around a central cane looking like an Edelweiss flower. Several of the canes show a little more variation than the usual simple cogs and stars from the Walsh and Arculus Glassworks. The second and third row from the outside are complex canes made by the grouping of bundles of canes. The most intriguing feature of this paperweight is the date 1848 with the letter B set above. In Baccarat dated weights, a B for Baccarat signature cane is also set above the date cane. This is only the second or third time I have seen or heard about this B cane in an English weight. The other piece was a large lamp stand with a millefiori base; it was signed and dated the same as this paperweight, but it also had a white rabbit cane. This lamp stand was attributed by the dealer to Whitefriars Glass. It is interesting to note that Mr. Parkes in his letter to the *Express* newspaper, says that "the old British craftsman, could very often surpass your Bigaglias and Saint Louis, etc." As Bigaglia and Saint Louis were nineteenth century producers of fine paperweights, this reference to them probably means that the English glassworkers had seen examples with dates included, and copied these antique French and Venetian paperweights.

Doorstop, c. 1930, Walsh-Walsh. $1500-2000. ***Courtesy of the Stone Gallery, Burford, England.***

A rare and interesting doorstop, almost 5.5" tall and made from five different paperweight set-ups. All the sides are different, although all the canes are of a simple construction. The canes can be found in other Walsh-Walsh paperweights and millefiori items. The set-ups are of only three rows around a small central cane, and are quite loosely packed, allowing some slippage and distortion. The colors are sharp and strong; this piece is in excellent condition, and was never used as a doorstop.

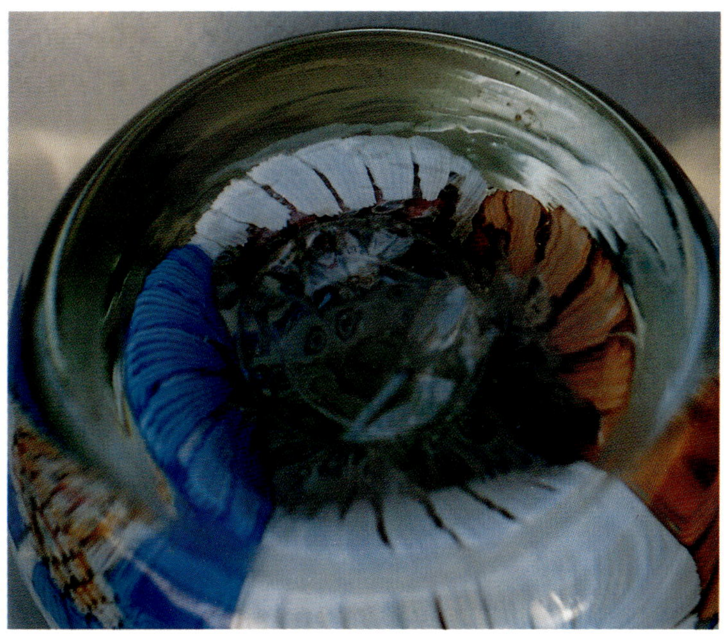

Base of Doorstop.

The base shows how the outside row has been pulled down and slightly under, to leave the cane ends showing rather untidily around the large broken pontil mark.

Candlestick, c. 1930, Walsh-Walsh. Height 8.1". $300-350. *Author's Collection.*

Three rows of loosely packed canes make up this concentric set up. The candle holder sits on a spiral twist of glass that is attached to the dome of the paperweight base. The sides of the dome have been damaged on the bottom edges and have been cut back by 0.5", otherwise the dome would have shown a gently rounded form.

Pair of Walsh-Walsh Candlesticks, c. 1930. Height 7.5". $600-750. *Author's Collection.*

A good pair of candlesticks. Although the bases are not matched, the green and white twists on the stem make them a pair. The canes are simple tubes and cogs that are set neatly around a central larger cog cane.

Base of Candlestick.

The central cane in this candlestick is a recognizable Walsh-Walsh cane. The four red petals are encased in white and set in a cog cane. The central part of this cane is used in other configurations and colors.

Walsh-Walsh Candlestick, c. 1930. Height 7.5". $300. *Author's Collection.*

A single candlestick from the same glassworks as the previous pair, with recognizable Walsh-Walsh canes. This candlestick was bought in San Diego, California at the 1997 P.C.A. convention.

Close-up of Candlestick.

This closer view shows a cane in the blue row, that has been described as a window cane, looking like the four panes of glass in a window. Also, two canes can be seen in the yellow row that are featured in many Walsh-Walsh paperweights and millefiori items, and are described in English collecting circles as the "seven and six" cane. This is a reference to English currency before decimalization, to describe seven shillings and sixpence. This "seven and six" cane can be found in other colors as well. In this candlestick there is a blue one out of view.

Walsh-Walsh Inkwell, Dated 1848, c. 1930. Height 5.25". Dia. 4.25". $1000-1250. *Author's Collection.*

This inkwell has many features that can aid identification of other Walsh-Walsh and Arculus pieces. The inkwell is almost as round as it is tall. This low bulbous appearance is quite different from many of the other inkwells in this book, and because of other identifying features linking it to Walsh-Walsh and Arculus, it would be reasonable to consider this shape to be the standard for the Walsh-Walsh/Arculus Glassworks. The shape is the same as the inkwell belonging to the Arculus family and so is the style of the numerals for the date canes. But the color of the date canes in this piece are lilac on white, and the Arculus family piece is blue on white. I feel that the slight differences in color and shape of the numerals are not that important, the differences being due to trial and error and what material the workers had when given the task of making date and other canes. Much of the variation in articles made by the same company must come down to the individual glassworker, unless the glassworks had a specified quantity, style, and order to produce for a customer. Also to be found in this piece are two rabbits, discreetly hidden on either side of the date cane, but several canes away. The sitting rabbits with large ears are white in clear glass, with one rabbit turned upside down. I have owned this piece for many years and had not noticed these two animals before. The seven rows of rather untidily placed canes are centred on the "seven and six" cane. This cane I have always thought to be some kind of signature cane as it might be interpreted as DL. To have this cane as the centre piece, and only to find it once in the cane set-up, could mean that someone was signing his work. The base has a recessed foot and a broken pontil mark.

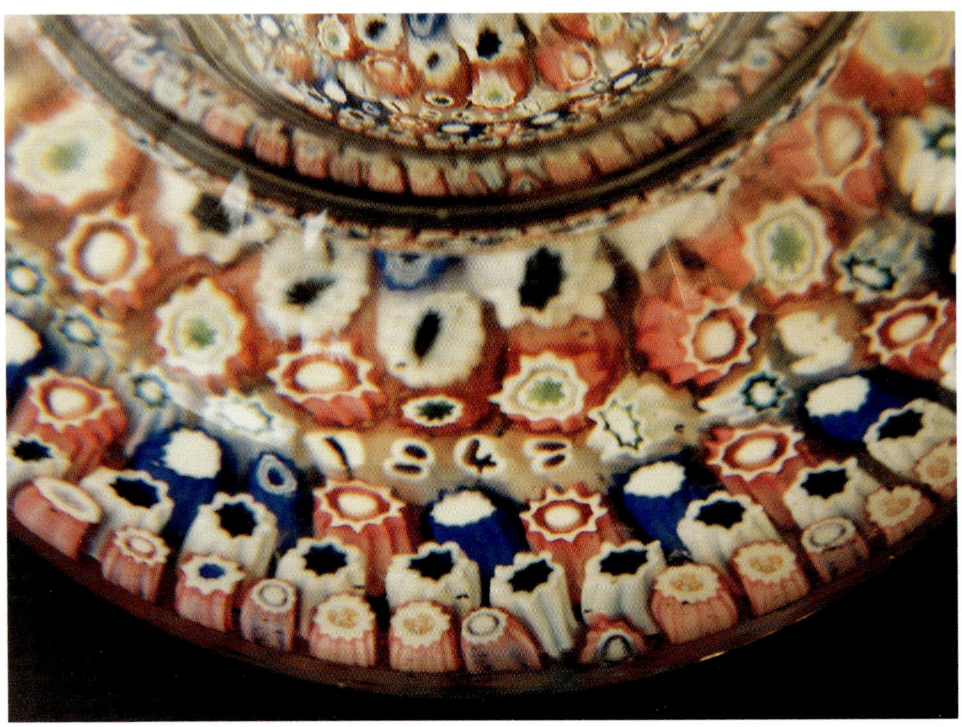

Close-up View of Inkwell.

Here can be seen one of the rabbits in the fourth row on the right of the date. The simple canes include a row of rarely seen black and white cogs. The 1848 date is set in the fourth row also, but Mr. Parkes, in his letter to the *Express* newspaper, says that he always set the date in the second row. Perhaps this one was made during the Arculus years.

Inkwell Stopper Showing "Seven and Six" Cane.

The cane that centres the stopper could be a signature cane DL, or 70, or, as it is now called by English collectors, the "seven and six cane;" fruiterers and fishmongers would write their produce prices in this fashion, using chisel pointed chalk or pens.

Close-up of "Seven and Six" cane in Concentric Walsh-Walsh Paperweight. *Courtesy of Terry and Hilary Johnson.*

Walsh-Walsh Inkwell, c. 1930. Height 4.75". Dia. 3.5". $600-750.
Courtesy of Mr. Skidmore.

This is a nice example from the Walsh-Walsh glassworks. The red, white, and blue canes are packed in tightly to prevent slippage. The canes are cogs and solid rods except for the window canes in the second row from the edge. The stopper is given extra height with the addition of a stem. The canes in the stopper mirror the base canes, and the inkwell sits on a recessed foot. As this piece was not dated and no attempt was made to antique the base by scratching, it could date this inkwell later than the fake dated pieces. The quality of the cane set-up and the depth of color is also better than many other examples. These inkwells and paperweights look very similar to the Whitefriars pieces of the 1970s and '80s, but the window cane puts it in the Walsh camp.

Base of Inkwell.

The base shows the canes drawn in towards the centre where the pontil rod was snapped off and left unground.

Walsh-Walsh Dated 1848 Concentric, c. 1930. Height 1.75". Dia. 3.25". $650-750. ***Courtesy of Mr. Skidmore.***

A low domed example with a good depth of color to the mainly simple canes. Again, this paperweight could have been produced as late as the early 1950s. It shows no signs of wear or damage, and is a definite improvement on some of the earlier paperweights attributed to the Walsh-Walsh factory. The date canes look almost black, but are a very dark purple on opal white. The profile shows the very low dome and cane cushion peculiar to the Arculus-Walsh glassworks.

Walsh-Walsh Paperweight, c. 1930. Height 1.75". Dia. 3.3". $900. ***Courtesy of The Portia Gallery, Chicago, Illinois.***

This six row concentric has, as its main attraction, a white rabbit. The Walsh-Walsh rabbits are normally well hidden but in this paperweight it sits right in the centre. In addition, the Walsh rabbits are normally seen only in profile, but this bunny sits so he can be seen only from above. Unfortunately, a small bubble sits on his back to partly obscure the view. However, a very nice example, closely packed in softly colored canes.

Base of Walsh-Walsh Paperweight.

The base shows the distinctive join where the two halves of the paperweight were mated together; the ridge can be easily felt with the finger tips. The pontil has been removed by deeply grinding into the base of the cane set-up. The sides of this type of paperweight can make the weight difficult to pick up by hand.

Base of Walsh-Walsh Paperweight.

The base shows the dealer's price sticker with the correct attribution. The canes are drawn to the centre and broken off with the pontil.

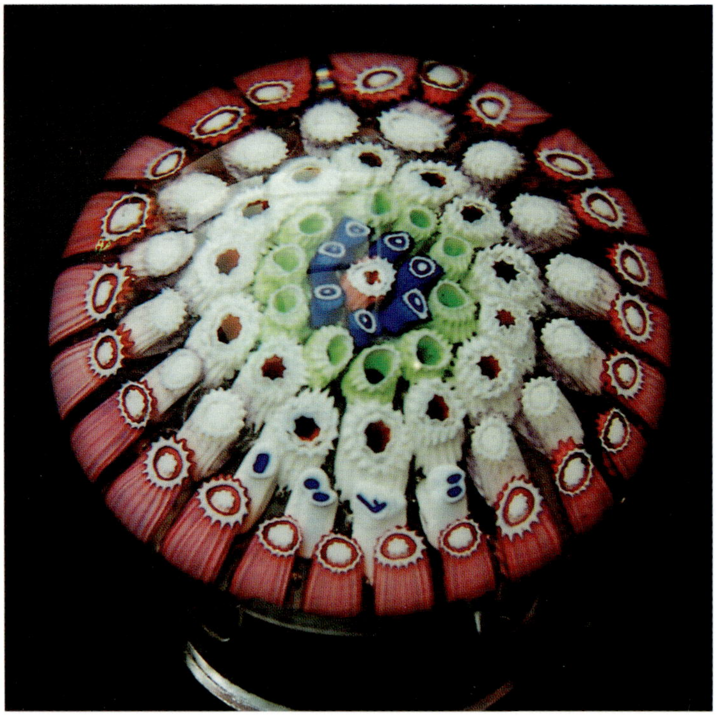

Walsh-Walsh Five Row Dated 1848 Paperweight, c. 1930. Height 1.75". Dia. 3.3". *Courtesy of Terry and Hilary Johnson.*

This striking example has, as the central cane, a red club on a white and red cog. The date stands out clearly in the second row. The base is hollow ground to remove pontil mark.

Walsh-Walsh Spill Holder, c. 1930. Height 4". Dia. 2". $150-175. *Author's Collection.*

A differently shaped body to the previous example with a rough pontil mark.

Pair of Walsh-Walsh Spill Holders, c. 1930. Height 4". Dia. 2.25". $300-350 *Courtesy of Terry and Hilary Johnson.*

A pair of spill or match holders, showing a base with rough pontil and a distinctive join where the two halves were put together. The flared holder sits on a paperweight base.

Walsh-Walsh Magnum Concentric with Diamond Facets, c. 1930. Dia. 4.25". $800-950. ***Collection of Karen & Paul Dunlop, © 1997 Papier Presse.***

A seven row concentric set around a large star cane. The paperweight is faceted all over except for the large window on the top. The diamond cutting gives the weight the appearance of being completely filled to capacity when the set-up size is actually only half the size of the weight. The paperweight is very similar to the modern Whitefriars, who also used this diamond cutting to great effect, but the cane in the fourth row from the centre is a Walsh-Walsh cane, usually described as a window cane. It is quite possible that Whitefriars were influenced in their designs by the glassworkers of Walsh. The movement of labour between glassworks was not uncommon, and in the depression of the 1930s workers who were laid off would travel for another job.

Walsh-Walsh, Four Row Concentric, c. 1930. Height 1.75". Dia. 3.5". $400-450. ***Courtesy of Terry and Hilary Johnson.***

A low dome example with four rows of simple canes around a central cog cane.

Walsh-Walsh, Five Row Concentric with 1950 Date. Height 1.6". Dia. 3.25". $400-500. ***Authors Collection.***

A paperweight such as this sloppy example would normally not get a second look, but this weight has a feature that is unique as far as I know: it has a 1950 date set amongst the canes. The figure 1 and another cog cane with sixteen teeth are the same as the canes held in the Broadfield House Museum, which were donated by a son of a former Walsh-Walsh worker. These canes, the low dome, and ground out base, identify it as Walsh-Walsh. The other numerals are white in clear glass, and have slipped during the picking-up process, probably because the canes are only loosely packed together.

Six Row Concentric. Height 2.1". Dia. 3.7". $400-500. *Courtesy of Terry and Hilary Johnson.*

Two rows of window canes can be viewed in this very good Walsh-Walsh paperweight. Also included is a nice lilac and white row of tube canes. The base is quite deeply indented with the rough pontil still visible. A distinctive ridge can be felt with the fingertips. A little detritus floats inside the otherwise clear glass dome.

Walsh-Walsh Bowl. Height 5". Dia. 6". $300-400. *Courtesy of Mr. & Mrs. Richard Giles.*

A well-formed bowl with millefiori canes in the base, to add interest to an everyday item.

Close-up of Bowl Canes.

Attractively set in the base, the concentric rows are centred on a well-known Walsh-Walsh cane. This cane, which resembles a window, appears in many of the firm's paperweights and other items. It may be that this cane is a distorted cross cane.

Two Dated 1848 Inkwells. Height 5". $800-900 each. ***Courtesy of The Sweetbriar Gallery, Helsby, England (Archive Photo).***

Both of these fine examples of dated inkwells were made in the 1930s. As fakes, the 1848 date canes gives added value to these pieces; without the date cane the pieces would be approximately $150 less in value but would still be keenly contested at auction, as they make wonderful decorative ornaments with a colorful history.

Spaced Millefiori on Lace Ground. Height 2". Dia. 3". $500-600.
Courtesy of the Sweetbriar Gallery, Helsby, England.

This is a possibly unique paperweight from Walsh-Walsh. At first quick glance it resembles an antique Baccarat, but hidden in the dark blue cane on the right hand side of the weight are two small, red on white letter B's. This seems to be another attempt to snare the unwary. Baccarat did sign many of their weights with a B, but the similarity ends there, as this weight, although interesting and rare, does not have the same quality and preciseness as an original Baccarat antique paperweight. Many modern paperweight makers have made this type of weight, with Perthshire Paperweights achieving the best results to date. Although we must give credit for this difficult design to a 1920-30 glasshouse, we cannot condone the attempt at deception.

Six Row Concentric. Height 1.75". Dia. 2.9". $400-500. *Courtesy of Dr. Geoffrey Dutton.*

This paperweight shows an untidiness that I associate with many of the Arculus set-ups, and may be from that period, just before Walsh-Walsh took over the factory. The outer rows begin quite neatly, but the inner rows have many mismatched canes. However, still quite a nice weight to look at. The base has been very deeply hollow ground, cutting into the bottom of the canes.

Walsh-Walsh Six Row Concentric with Twelve Rabbit Canes. Height 1.9". Dia. 3". $500-750. *Courtesy of Bill Volkman.*

Walsh-Walsh usually hid their rabbit canes with one or two in a row of similar colored canes, but in this weight they used twelve bunnies in a row of blue and white cog canes. They are quite difficult to see as the glass dome is striated and the rabbit canes are not too sharp and slightly distorted. Another odd cane is the centre feature cane which is a white block with the figure 1 in red.

Chapter Ten

Stevens and Williams

Brierley Hill, Stourbridge, England

Messrs. Stevens and Williams were the founders of a glass manufacturing business in 1776. The company grew in size and stature in the ownership of family members until 1930. At that time, the company was taken over by the much larger business of Royal Brierley Crystal, a company that is still a major producer of fine crystal at the present time. Their production of tableware is of such quality that commissions are undertaken from governments and Royal Houses worldwide. From the beginning, the company made table glass, including wine glasses with colored spiral twists in the stems.

Some of these glasses are still on display at the company's private museum, and show single and multi-colored twists of cane in the stems, including, white, red, blue, and a rare yellow color. The museum, which is only open by appointment, is run by a former Master engraver and glassblower, Mr. Sam Thompson, born 1909. Sam has spent all his working life with the company, working alongside the glassblowers and engravers. As curator of the museum, he has an intimate knowledge of most of the pieces in the collection, which must now number many hundreds of the most exquisite nature. Many of the more elaborately engraved vases were blown as a blank and then engraved by Sam. He was also Chief Designer, and, as did the company from its beginning, he kept meticulous records of every production piece made by the factory.

Anne Anderson, Chair of the Cambridge Paperweight Circle, and I were invited by Royal Brierley Crystal to visit the Museum, interview Sam Thompson, and examine the company records going back to 1776. Our aim was to try and establish whether paperweights were made by the company in the nineteenth century or the beginning of the twentieth century. Anne Anderson had informed me that during research into an article she was writing for the Paperweight Collectors Association, she had come across a reference to a Mr. H.S. Williams. Mr. Williams had been thanked by Maciver Percival in his book *The Glass Collector*, for his assistance in describing the decorative process, the making of millefiori rods, and the cutting and drawing out of the same. Mr. Williams is quoted as saying "Messrs. Stevens and Williams of Brierley Hill, Stourbridge, did not let the old processes die out, and still retain the skills, moulds, and appliances that were in use a hundred years ago, and that reproductions are still being made now."

A close examination of the company's book of designs, which are all beautifully drawn by hand, did not reveal any paperweights, inkwells, scent bottles, or any item with a millefiori content at all. Twists of colored cane have in the past been described as "millefiori" by various writers of bygone years, and it is possible that the reference to "millefiori rods" in *The Glass Collector* were rods of twisted glass to be used in wine glass stems. The company has without a doubt made paperweights, but not on a production basis. The glassworkers were actively encouraged to test their skills using glass canes that were not required at the end of the work shift. Sam Thompson recalls that most of the glass workers would use the leftovers to make gifts for friends and family.

The two paperweights illustrated in this chapter were made at the factory by an unknown worker, and purchased by Mr. Gilbert Hill who was a Director of the company. Mr. Hill was responsible for sales during his sixty years with the company, and informed me that he knew of many friggers being made with the company's approval, but as he was in charge of sales from the 1930s he could assure me that no millefiori paperweight production took place. He has in his possession two friggers that were made in the 1930s that he had bought from the factory. The factory disposed of oddments of glass by placing them on a "job" table and allowing workers to purchase items at cut prices to clear them out. Cut and clear glass weights and menu holders were produced as limited production runs for special orders, but none had millefiori canes included. William Swingewood, who was a noted lampworker, worked at the factory in the 1930s and is well remembered by Sam Thompson and Gilbert Hill. Both commented that he was quite capable of producing paperweights, and probably made a small quantity to test his skills. Some of his lampworked animals are placed inside the blown stems of vases, bowls, and hunting cups and are displayed in the company museum.

Royal Brierley Crystal, Stourbridge, England. Photographed in 1997, the factory is still owned by the Williams family, and is producing fine glassware for domestic use and export the world over.

Honeybourne Cottage.

A cottage was built in the grounds of the factory to house an engraving department, and it was here that copies of the famous Portland Vase were made. Blanks were made by the Richardson factory, also based in Stourbridge, and engraved by John Northwood. The tools used in the cutting and engraving are still with the museum, which is now housed in this cottage and named Honeybourne. The original Portland Vase was damaged in the 1920s by a man who went berserk in the museum where the vase was being exhibited. The vase was rebuilt and is still on display at the Victoria and Albert Museum in London.

In the museum, there is a cupful of millefiori canes given to the curator by a glassworker named Sid Baker, many years ago. The canes, which bear a strong resemblance to the Scottish style of Vasart and Strathern, gave us hope that there may be something we could tie to the factory. On close inspection, several parts of these canes are in fact parts of whole canes which can be matched to the selection of canes illustrated in the *Ysart Glass*[1] book. On closer questioning, it seems that several workers came from Scotland to learn glass making techniques in the 1960s and '70s. The Royal Brierley factory had close business links with Caithness Glass and Teachers whiskey. Teachers took over the Vasart Glass factory in 1964 and renamed the company Strathern Glass. This company has made many thousands of paperweights, and this would seem to explain how the museum acquired the canes which were thought to have been made by themselves. Sam Thompson remembers quite clearly various workers experimenting with paperweights, and described in detail how the canes were inserted into weights. The canes were not set into iron moulds as most modern day manufacturers would do; the pieces of cane would be lightly inserted into a clay mould or mound and then picked up by lowering the soft glass crown onto the canes, and reworking at the glory hole to shape the weight.

One last piece of information given to me by Sam was that they had a working relationship with the Arculus and Walsh-Walsh glassworks, who were both making paperweights in the 1920-30s. He could not elaborate on the precise nature of the relationship, but thought that canes and rods were sold to them when an overproduction meant that the surplus could be sold off. The factory now buys its rod and cane requirements from Germany.

Wine Goblet. Height 7.25".

Included in the blown enclosure of this baluster wine goblet is a huntsman, holding aloft a fox after the kill. Dressed in a traditional foxhunting red jacket and black boots, the figure was lampworked by William Swingewood who worked at the Brierley Hill factory in the 1930s. This piece is on display in the factory museum.

Wine Goblet. Height 7.25".

A baluster goblet showing the fox alive before the chase; also by William Swingewood, it is displayed in the museum.

Paperweight Frigger, Made by an Unknown Worker at Stevens and Williams, Royal Brierley Crystal, Stourbridge, c. 1930. Dia. 3.25". *Courtesy of Gilbert Hill.*

This is a paperweight made by an unknown worker during the 1930s-40s. The weight shows considerable wear to the crown and base, and has an annealing crack which completely encircles the weight. The eight lengths of spiral cane, in red, dark blue, and white, are laid out in a wagon wheel style, and encircled by similar lengths of cane to make the outer rim of the wagon wheel. The wheel is set above a ground of gray sand-like material. Very little monetary value can be set against this weight as it contains a serious crack and has little artistic content. The weight however has significant value as it was definitely made by Stevens and Williams - Royal Brierley Crystal.

Profile of Paperweight Frigger, Height 2.75".

The side view of this frigger shows a very high profile with the canes set high into the crown of the weight. The base is unusual in that it has been hollow ground to remove the pontil mark, and then the base has been ground flat to leave a large dimple in the centre.

Paperweight Frigger, Stevens and Williams - Royal Brierley Crystal, Made by Unknown Worker, c. 1945. *Courtesy of Gilbert Hill.*

This Spitfire airplane has adventurine on its wings as camouflage. The roundel Royal Airforce markings on the wings are small pieces of glass set on the wings and are not millefiori canes. The plane is flying over a ground of spattered glass fragments and is a reasonable representation of the aircraft. The base has a rough pontil and shows considerable wear. The weight could have been made during the 1939-45 war or just after.

Millefiori canes held by Brierley Hill Glassworks Museum.

These canes, held by the museum, could have originated from a Scottish source. The canes bear a striking resemblance to canes produced by the Ysart brothers during their various careers at different Scottish glass houses. The centres of several of these canes do appear in some canes illustrated in the Ysart Glass book. It would not be surprising if friggers made by the workers at the end of their work shift included these Scottish canes. The canes were given to the museum by a shop floor worker. Many unusual weights, with no easily identifiable attribution, appear on the local antique and flea market circuit in the Birmingham area. I would be interested in hearing of any weights held by readers that contain these canes.

Among these canes you will see a small clay sulphide of a face, which was modeled by Sam Thompson and used to decorate vases and goblets produced by Royal Brierley Crystal. These inclusions were nearly all one off, or special pieces made to order. The museum does have in its possession an Apsley Pellat sulphide which is encased in glass and was part of a vase which was broken by accident. The piece was irrecoverable but the sulphide was kept as a souvenir.

Mr. Sam Thompson, born 1909. Curator of the Royal Brierley Crystal Museum (formerly the Brierley Hill Glassworks Museum).

Sam Thompson was shown a selection of English paperweights of unidentifiable makers in the hope he might be able to recognize a paperweight or a style. Although they all looked familiar to him, he could not say with any certainty that they were made by this factory. He has made paperweights himself but said that no two friggers ever looked the same; it all had to do with the various materials left at the end of the day.

A Sulphide head and shoulders by Apsley Pellat, c. 1830. Recovered from a broken vase.

Close-up of Complex Cane. ***Courtesy of Brierley Hill Glassworks Museum.***

Cane with "88". ***Courtesy of Brierley Hill Glassworks Museum.***

Included amongst the canes were two that had the figure 2 and a cane that looks like an 88, although it has been pointed out that this could be four close circles. Judge for yourself.

Clay Mould. ***Courtesy of Brierley Hill Glassworks Museum.***

The horse head clay mould was also sculpted by Sam Thompson, who used the heads produced to decorate hunting cups and goblets.

Close-up of Complex Cane. ***Courtesy of Brierley Hill Glassworks Museum.***

Chapter Eleven

Inkwells

Inkwells and scent bottles with a millefiori content have probably been made since the late nineteenth century. However, as the manufacturers never kept to one distinct pattern or shape that could be reliably identified with their glasshouse, the attribution of these pieces is difficult. The practice of keeping accurate records and pattern books was not one of the English glass industry's strong points. This may have been because many of the firms were small and may not have survived in business for long. Several of the major glassworks, with histories that go back 150 years and more, did keep some records. However, probably because these millefiori objects were only produced as a minor sideline, the information available to the dedicated researcher is very limited.

Several references have survived, and can give us an indication and guide to who made what. The earliest reference with a drawing is by H.G. Richardson & Sons, of Stourbridge. This line drawing shows a bulbous shaped body with a flared lip and inverted footed base. The canes are set low into the base of the inkwell, which shows five rows of canes. A paperweight shaped stopper sits on the top, also with millefiori canes. It would be reasonable to assume, with this documented evidence, that all inkwells with this shape could be attributed to the Richardson glassworks. Unfortunately, it would be wrong to make this assumption because a millefiori inkwell on display in the Birmingham City Art Gallery has a profile that is nothing like this bulbous shape, but has canes within that can be linked to Richardson. This latter piece is tall and elegant and deeply faceted on six sides with a matching stopper, and with canes that match those in an inkwell and paperweight with the same shape as the ones in the pattern books. I have assumed that by matching the shape and construction of paperweights and inkwells in these pattern books dated 1913 with paperweights held by myself and other collectors, that the canes contained in these pieces could be used to identify Richardson made pieces. The paperweights match the known shape and weight exactly, so if this identification can be relied on, then the process of attributing weights and inkwells becomes that much easier. We now have two inkwells with matching canes, one in the Birmingham Art Gallery and one in my own collection, with totally different shapes but with matching canes, and also paperweights with canes that match those in the inkwells. This progression of identification is all we have to work with at the present time.

The next authenticated evidence is a picture in *The Pottery Gazette and Glass Trade Review*, dated 1945. The picture shows two paperweights and an inkwell by James Powell & Sons (Whitefriars), Ltd. The likeness to the Richardson inkwell is remarkable; the only difference between the two pieces is that the Whitefriars inkwell has slightly taller sides. The foot on the Whitefriars piece cannot be seen clearly enough to determine whether there is a recessed foot or not, as on the Richardson inkwell.

There is also the inkwell belonging to the Arculus family. Although this piece is no longer available for photographing, the illustration in the 1995 P.C.A. Bulletin shows an inkwell that looks to be the mirror image of the one illustrated in the Richardson pattern book. With regard to the dated examples, of which only 1848 ever appears, we must remember that both Arculus and Walsh-Walsh were producing "antique" inkwells and paperweights in the 1920s. These inkwells could have been copies of the Richardson inkwell with 1848 added for authenticity. The Arculus company were certainly placing the 1848 canes in their pieces as early as 1922 and maybe earlier than that.

The final documented evidence is a reference in a Whitefriars catalogue produced in 1938; this shows a footed, 5-inch tall inkwell, with steep sides and a low domed stopper in a tall neck. Alongside this piece is a high dome, 3-inch diameter paperweight, with millefiori canes rising high into the crown of the weight. The inkwell is priced at 25 shillings (50 cents), and the paperweight is priced at 15 shillings (30 cents).

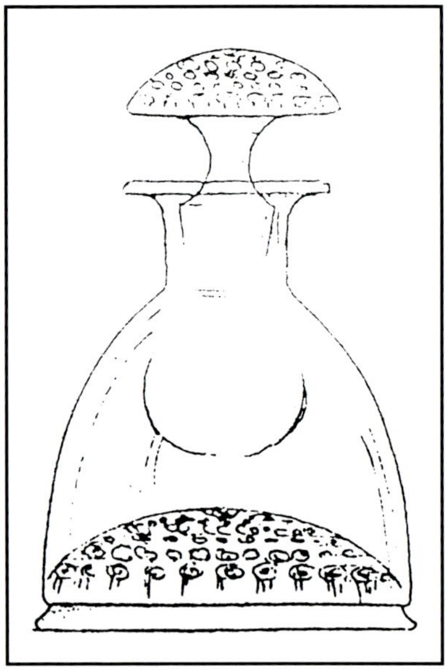

Whitefriars Inkwell, c. 1930.

This line drawing was taken from a Whitefriars catalogue, in use until 1938.

Inkwell by Unknown Maker. Height 3.5". Dia. 3.6". $300-400.
Courtesy of Terry and Hilary Johnson.

Inkwells come in all shapes and sizes, as demonstrated by this very pretty inkwell with a row of flower-like canes. Many inkwells do not survive with their original stoppers, if they ever had one; a replacement that matches is almost impossible to find. The body of the inkwell is larger in diameter than the height, making it very stable.

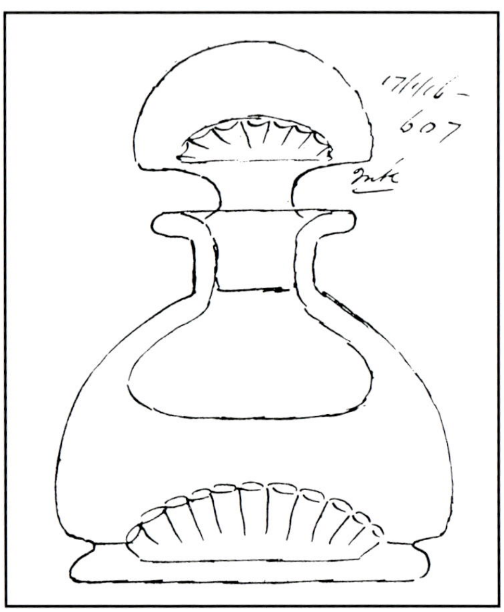

Design for an Inkwell by H.G. Richardson & Sons, Dated 1916.

This bulbous and footed inkwell was taken from the Richardson pattern book, dated 1916.

Base of Inkwell.

The set-up of the canes is relatively small in comparison to the size of the body but the magnifying properties of the glass enhance the size superbly.

Inkwell by Unknown Maker. Height 3.5". Dia. 3.6". $300-400. *Author's Collection.*

This inkwell is from the same manufacturer as the previous piece. The outside two rows of canes are the same. The bright yellow canes in the centre are similar to canes that are quite common in 1930s Chinese paperweights. The canes are set untidily around a red and white cog cane. The base shows only medium wear with a rough pontil mark.

Base of Cone Shaped Inkwell.

This base has been finished off perfectly, and makes an attractive part of the whole piece. The construction is very precise and similar to the finish found on Bacchus paperweights. The canes are drawn to the centre and the pontil mark is removed by lightly grinding. The base has a recessed foot.

Cone Shaped Inkwell with Matching Stopper, Unknown Maker. Height 3.75". Dia. 4.3". $500-750. *Author's Collection.*

An inkwell with a very distinctive cone shape. The very wide base and style are similar to a ship's decanter. The red and white canes are simply made, but set out precisely to make an attractive piece.

Cone Shaped Inkwell with Matching Stopper, Unknown Maker. Height 3.75". Dia. 4.3". $500-750. *Author's Collection.*

From the same glasshouse as the previous example with a good swirl stopper. This type of shape is not as common as the bulbous shaped inkwells. The bases show a good amount of wear and may be from an earlier period than the Arculus, Richardson, and Walsh-Walsh pieces.

Footed Inkwell, Part of a Pair, Unknown Maker. Height 4.2". Dia. 3.6". $400-500 (single). *Author's Collection.*

Five rows of canes around a star cane; tightly packed canes prevent slippage when picking up the cane set-up. Apart from being a pair, there are no canes in these inkwells to make them stand out from the rest.

Ladies Inkwell or Scent Bottle with Victoria Heads, Unknown Maker. Height 3.5". Dia. 3". $750-1000. *Author's Collection.*

Two white on green and two white on clear glass Victoria Heads make this a very interesting bottle. A small close packed cushion of canes is well magnified to look as though the bottle is full, when in reality the canes only fill half the bottle. Some of the canes are very complex and look very similar in color and construction to those used by Bacchus. Open ruffles and eighteen teeth cog canes can also be found that may tie it to the Bacchus Glassworks. This may be a unique inkwell, as, despite many inquiries, no similar size with this type of quality cane seems to exist. I would be pleased to hear of another example. The base is footed with the canes drawn towards the centre. This inkwell was purchased from a Birmingham street market in a very distressed condition. The rim had been completely broken off, and the foot had been damaged so badly that the glass repairers cut into the base to remove all the sharp and ragged edges. This is one of my favourite pieces.

Seven Row Concentric Inkwell, Unknown Maker. Height 5.5". Dia. 3.75". $500-600. ***Author's Collection.***

The stopper is not quite the matching piece for this bulbous inkwell. Although the canes in the base and stopper are almost the same, the colors do not match. The two pieces look as though they are from the same glasshouse but could have been mismatched by a careless packer. The canes are drawn beneath and to the centre of the footed base to make for an attractive finish.

Inkwell with a Row Of Victoria Heads, Unknown Maker. Height 4.6". Dia. 2.25". $700-800. ***Author's Collection.***

These small inkwells are normally referred to as ladies inkwells. There are only three rows of canes in this piece but the outside row is made up of green heads on white ground to make it different from the rest. The base has a rough pontil and sits on an inverted foot.

Six Row Concentric Inkwell, Unknown Maker. Height 4.2". Dia. 3.75". $500-600. ***Author's Collection.***

This inkwell is almost circular in shape. The canes are neatly arranged with a matching stopper. Rough pontil.

Inkwell, Unknown Maker, Nineteenth Century. Height 4". Dia. 3.5". $400-500. *Collection of Mr. & Mrs. Giles.*

This very attractive inkwell does not contain millefiori canes but is full of colored twists and glass chippings. Probably made at the end of the day's workings as a test piece to further the workman's skills. A very unusual low shape and possibly unique as a frigger.

Inkwell with Four Concentric Rows. Height 3.5". Dia. 3". $300-400. *Courtesy of Mr. & Mrs. Richard Giles.*

A bulbous shape to this inkwell, with four rows of red, white, and blue simple cog canes. A deep inverted foot adds a little style and interest to this piece.

Bulbous Inkwell from Unknown Maker. Height 4.1". Dia. 3.5". $300-400. *Author's Collection.*

A five row concentric with the canes loosely packed, which has allowed them to move during the making process. Red and white solid cogs and pale blue tubes surround a central green and white, large cog cane. The base has a broken pontil mark.

Close Packed Inkwell. Height 3.2". Dia. 3.3". $250-350. ***Courtesy of Mr. & Mrs. Richard Giles.***

Amongst the tubes, cogs and mixed simple canes, sits a club cane to add a little interest. This piece has a broken top and a foot with a rough pontil. The top has been reground to remove dangerous sharp edges. Still a nice piece for a desktop.

Four Row Concentric Inkwell. Height 4.75". Dia. 3". $500-700. ***Courtesy of Anne Anderson.***

A bulbous body on this strikingly colored inkwell from Arculus or Walsh-Walsh. A deep foot on the base with lilac and white, red and white, and blue and white cog canes, around a larger cog as a centre.

Inkwell with Copper Lid. Height 3.5". Dia. 2.2". $400-500. ***Courtesy of Anne Anderson.***

Only simple canes in this attractive inkwell but the added attraction of the copper lid makes it quite rare. Its quite possible that this inkwell was made in the 1850s, but with no documentary evidence from any English producers, it will have to remain anonymous, with the date of manufacture still a mystery

Broken Inkwell. ***Courtesy of Anne Anderson.***

A seriously damaged inkwell can be repaired. Damage to the neck and lip can often be repaired by a glass repair shop, which can remove the damaged neck by grinding flat to the top of the body and gluing on a new neck often salvaged from damaged decanters. Modern glass glues applied by experts can be invisible to the eye. The value of the repaired piece would be less than an original but better than a sharp and ragged edge.

Broken Inkwell. ***Courtesy of Anne Anderson.***

This inkwell has had the top ground down to remove the damaged neck and lip. The alternative could be to remove all of the waste glass and make it into a paperweight. Many strange shaped paperweights turn up with hardly any dome in comparison to its diameter. In many cases this would indicate a repair job to an inkwell.

Broken Inkwell. ***Private Collection.***

This inkwell shows signs of quality in the cane set-up and faceting. The circular facets encompass the inkwell completely, allowing the viewer to observe the pale blue and pink canes, all set around a red and white large cog cane in a tube. The lip on the top has been damaged and removed. This inkwell could be attributed to Richardson for the quality setting and faceting.

Base of Broken Inkwell.

The canes are drawn to the centre with several not quite making it, but overall the base is well finished with the pontil removed by grinding.

Five Row Concentric. Height 6". $500-650.
Courtesy of The Sweetbriar Gallery, Helsby, England. (Archive Photo)

The following selection of inkwells were all probably made in the Stourbridge area. The canes and set-ups are all very precise, unlike the other known makers of inkwells, Walsh-Walsh and Arculus, who allowed slippage of canes in most of their pieces. It is quite possible that all of the better made pieces were indeed made by the Richardson Glassworks around 1910. The shapes can vary, as most were made freehand.

Matched Set of Paperweights and Inkwell. Inkwell: Height 6". Paperweights: Height 2.75". Dia. 4". $1800-2000 (for set). ***Courtesy of The Sweetbriar Gallery, Helsby, England. (Archive Photo)***

A stunning set of magnum paperweights and inkwell set. These complete sets are now extremely rare, as most get damaged and are sold off as individual pieces. With the addition of another gather of glass the paperweights become inkwells.

Six Row Concentric Inkwell. Height 5". $600-700. ***Courtesy of The Sweetbriar Gallery, Helsby, England.(Archive Photo)***

This inkwell is almost certainly made by Richardson of Stourbridge. The outer row of canes look the same as in paperweights and inkwells attributed to this quality maker.

Six Row Concentric Inkwell. Height 5.5". $600-700. ***Courtesy of the Sweetbriar Gallery, Helsby, England. (Archive Photo)***

Strong coloring makes this a striking example. The outer rows of red cog canes really make this inkwell stand out from the rest. A fine and well made piece. Matching stopper.

Five Row Concentric Inkwell. Height 5.5". $600-700. ***Courtesy of The Sweetbriar Gallery, Helsby, England. (Archive Photo)***

Almost identical in size and shape to the previous inkwell. This one has canes colored in lilacs and blues, all in simple cogs and solid rods. Matching stopper.

Close Packed Millefiori Inkwell. Height 5". $750-850. ***Courtesy of The Sweetbriar Gallery, Helsby, England. (Archive Photo)***

This is a superb inkwell with a large variety of mainly pastel colored canes. Using predominantly solid rods, cogs, and the occasional hollow tube, interest is maintained wherever you look. The stopper, although not millefiori, may well be the original for this piece as it looks and fits perfectly.

Six Row Concentric Inkwell. Height 6". $600-700. ***Courtesy of The Sweetbriar Gallery, Helsby, England. (Archive Photo)***

This inkwell has the same coloring as that favoured by the Whitefriars glasshouse, and although unsigned or dated, it may be from this glassworks made in the early 1970s.

Five Row Concentric Inkwell. Height 5.5". Dia. 4.5". $650-700. ***Courtesy of Dr. Geoffrey Dutton.***

The lilac colors make this a striking example. The simply made canes are all set around a large dark blue cog cane. The bulbous shape and coloring puts it in the Arculus or Walsh-Walsh camp.

Five Row Concentric Inkwell with Brass Top. Height 4.75". $750-850. ***Courtesy of Bill Volkman.***

An unknown maker made this quality piece. The brass top is hinged to allow access to the inside and looks to be original to the piece. The canes are of a simple construction but precisely set around a central cog cane, which has a rarely seen row of powder blue canes around it. The inkwell is footed with a rough pontil.

Concentric Inkwell and Matching Paperweight. Height 5.5". $1250-1400. ***Courtesy of Bill Volkman.***

This is a very unusual set which may have been made around the early 1900s. The cutting looks very similar to the inkwell in the Birmingham Art Gallery and Museum, England. The deep vertical cutting and the nicely set canes place the set almost certainly in the Richardson Glassworks category.

Chapter Twelve

Whitefriars

James Powell (1774-1840)

James Powell purchased a glasshouse, built in 1680 on the grounds of a demolished monastery occupied by a Carmelite order of the White Friars. Powell bought this well established glasshouse in 1834, and although his main business was the importation and distribution of wines, his business acumen was such that the glass business continued to thrive despite the glass tax still being in place. This tax was a serious burden to glass producers and was not repealed until 1845. After the repeal, Powell set about recovering business lost to foreign imports. James Powell & Sons were one of seventeen English glasshouses exhibiting at the 1851 Great Exhibition in London, where they won a prize for their fine crystal and colored glass; although they must have had a fine display of their wares, no mention is made of paperweights or millefiori. The official catalogue of the Exhibition pays attention to the influence of "The Venetian Style" and mentions Bacchus, Rice Harris (Islington Glassworks) of Birmingham, Richardson, and Greathead & Green of Stourbridge, who all displayed wares in "The Venetian" manner.

As one of England's most prominent and successful glasshouses, Whitefriars must have been aware of products that were so successful for the foreign glasshouses of Baccarat, Clichy, and Saint Louis, all of which by this time were flooding the stationers and fancy goods shops in England with paperweights. They must surely have experimented with the techniques of paperweight manufacture, even if they never went into volume production. As early as 1830, paperweights were being made in England with a sulphide inclusion by Apsley Pellatt who was an authority on the fusion of glass. Around 1840 Pellatt was lecturing at the Royal College of Chemistry in London on how to make glass in the "Venetian Style," and went on to publish his book, *The Curiosities of Glassmaking*, in 1849. In this book he describes, with illustrations and descriptive techniques, the making of filigree canes and millefiori. But even if Whitefriars knew all this, there was never a mention in any archive material, nor were any documented pieces attributed to this glasshouse in the 1845-1850 period, when so many paperweights were being bought by the English public. Whitefriars continued to exhibit nationally and internationally and won many prizes, but no catalogue or record mentions paperweights.

During the last quarter of the nineteenth century, Whitefriars were greatly influenced by the "Venetian Style," and used filigree twists of colored cane in many of their designs. Whitefriars has been credited with dated paperweights and inkwells from 1848, with no evidence to support this except myth and hearsay. The first documented evidence for millefiori production is in the form of a vase held in the Museum of London, Wall, London. This shaped glass vase has several pieces of millefiori canes embedded in the sides of the piece, and can definitely be attributed to Whitefriars in 1877. To date, this is the earliest piece so far recorded with millefiori inclusions. However, this is not to say they did not make paperweights or inkwells, but only that there is no direct link to the classic period at the present time. It would be unreasonable to say that a major glass producer, with a history as long as Whitefriars, never made paperweights, but the paperweights and inkwells known to be made by them (from the 1930s to the 1970s) never included a date cane. The paperweights and inkwells with the 1848 date canes attributed to Whitefriars were made by Arculus and Walsh-Walsh in the 1920s and '30s. If Whitefriars were making millefiori objects with a date cane in 1848, then surely it would be logical to have continued such a practice, which adds interest and value to paperweights and inkwells. Even if the production were of a limited and interrupted nature and spread over many years, I feel certain that date canes would have been added, had this been their normal way of making weights and inkwells. The 1848 dated pieces were a probable response to the increased awareness of paperweight collecting and the increasing values in the early part of the twentieth century. We now know that these 1848 dated pieces supposedly by Whitefriars deceived and took advantage of a naive collecting public. As there is no known, authentic attribution of a single antique paperweight that makes the link to Whitefriars, it is impossible to identify one of the many unknown "English style" weights that are not

Whitefriars Vase, 1877, © *Courtesy of The Museum of London. London Wall, London.*

This magnificent opal blue vase is on display at the Museum of London, and can be linked to James Powell (Whitefriars) in 1877. In 1876 a man named Bibby was a glassblower at the Whitefriars glasshouse, and it was noted by James Powell that this man (Bibby) was experimenting with "flower canes," placing slices into vases and jugs. Bibby left the company in 1877. The engraved vase has six millefiori canes set into the glass sides as flowerheads in the fern-like leaves. The centre of the canes has a white cross set into a red cog with eighteen teeth. The only other nineteenth century known paperweight maker to use an eighteen cog cane was George Bacchus. A similar eighteen cog cane can be seen in the ladies inkwell shown in Chapter Eleven of this book. Did Whitefriars use Bacchus canes in this vase as a test piece? This vase was an obvious success, but maybe Whitefriars had problems with the compatibility of canes for insertion into vases and gave up this design. The cane slices are approximately 3/16" thick and the glass vase walls only 1/8" thick. This is certainly an extremely rare, if not unique, millefiori vase.

Richardson, Arculus or Walsh-Walsh and label it as "Whitefriars." It is only in the 1920s that documents have been produced that show paperweights and inkwells made by Whitefriars. Even remarks made by the Whitefriars company, in a catalogue produced in the 1970s, refer to a dated "1848 Whitefriars inkwell, made by themselves and reproduced for today's collectors," probably refers to an Arculus or Walsh-Walsh piece that they must have seen or been told about. I am reasonably confident that many small production runs and friggers have been produced over the last 150 years or so, but which are the genuine antiques (if any?) and what do they look like? What canes and colors did they use? These unknown weights and inkwells are probably in this book somewhere, but I have not been able to put a finger on one with any certainty as yet.

Production of paperweights was temporarily suspended during the Second World War. In February 1945 *The Pottery Gazette and Glass Trade Review* published a picture of a pair of millefiori paperweights and an inkwell, describing them as having "colored enamel decoration." The inkwell seems to have changed to a more bulbous shape, with the paperweights being not quite as tall as in the previous known line drawing. The production of paperweights was increased with the arrival of Geoffrey Baxter in 1954 as assistant designer to William Wilson, the then managing director and chief designer of Whitefriars. Until Baxter's arrival, most modern paperweight production seems to have been made from solid glass, with color and bubble added for decoration, although occasionally they did produce special orders as can be seen with the 1951 Triplex weight. This commemorative piece was produced for another glassmaking concern who specialized in non-decorative commercial glass, Triplex Ltd, and who are still trading to day. Several unmarked paperweights that are almost identical to the "Triplex" weight were produced in the following years. The 1970s, with the designs of Geoffrey Baxter, brought Whitefriars to the forefront of paperweight making, and in the following years they produced Christmas and limited edition paperweights and inkwells that were the match of any modern paperweight of the day. Many of these designs were inspired by the craftsmanship of Ray Annenberg. Ray made the canes and was a paperweight maker with Whitefriars until the firm closed due to insufficient orders in 1980.

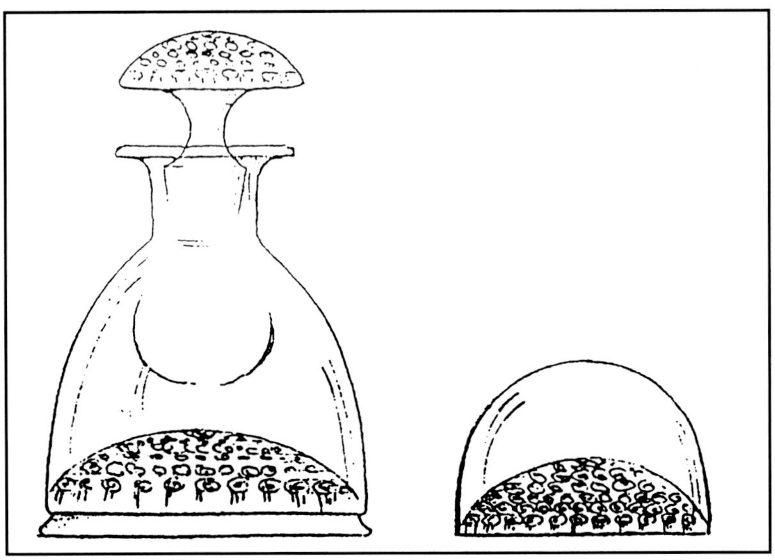

Early Whitefriars Inkwell and Paperweight from c. 1930 Glass Catalogue.

This drawing is probably the earliest known inkwell and paperweight from Whitefriars. The catalogue it appears in is undated but has the address of the glassworks as Wealdstone, Middlesex, London, premises which they occupied from 1923. This type of line drawn catalogue was in use until 1939, so these two items could have been made at any time during this period. The 3" diameter, approximately 2" high dome of the paperweight and the steeply rising sides of the 5" inkwell should help with identification, but with so many English pieces following the same style and shape it is not as simple as it seems. Arculus, who produced inkwells and paperweights before 1922, also made paperweights with this high dome, to achieve maximum magnification of the millefiori canes. The low dome of the stopper is also reminiscent of Arculus pieces. The cost of the inkwell is given as 25— shillings ($5.00), and the paperweight as 15— shillings ($3.00) (calculated when the English £1 was equal to $4 US).

Photograph from *The Pottery Gazette And Glass Trade Review*, Feb. 1945. *Courtesy of The Broadfield House Glass Museum, Kingswinford, England.*

This photograph has the description, "Ink bottle and paperweights, with colored enamel decoration." Millefiori canes were often described as enamel in the early twentieth century by writers on glass subjects, and many old glassworkers still use this terminology today. The pieces all show the typical concentric set-ups used by all the English manufacturers, four or five rows of canes around a simple large cog cane.

Spiral Weight. Height 2.3". Dia. 2.9". $100-150. *Author's Collection.*

Spiral paperweights were made after the Second World War, and this one, with its red, white, and blue national colors, may have been made for Queen Elizabeth's Coronation in 1953. The base is hollow ground with no basal ring.

Faceted Paperweight. Height 3". $300-400. *Courtesy of Terry and Hilary Johnson.*

Whitefriars had a very extensive cutting and engraving department, and utilized these facilities in the majority of their work. Paperweights could be faceted in numerous different styles. Of the fifty paperweights on offer in the following catalogue only five are not faceted.

Triplex Paperweight. Height 1.7". Dia. 3". $300-400. *Author's Collection.*

This paperweight is possibly one of the earliest of the modern day weights from Whitefriars. Pleased with the reaction to this paperweight from Triplex, for whom a small production of advertising gift weights were made, management and workers were encouraged to submit designs for more. This weight has the words "Triplex 1951" engraved on the central cane. Ray Annenberg described to the Cambridge Paperweight Circle, in a talk he gave on Whitefriars in 1995, that the central cane is a solid white rod dipped in a thin coat of dark blue, then the words are etched through the outer layer to reveal the white core. It would seem that this is the earliest recorded paperweight from Whitefriars with a date cane. This method for dating canes was never used after this paperweight was made. The base of this weight shows the central cane reaching to the base where it forms part of the rough pontil mark. The ridge mark where the button was picked up is very distinctive, even more so than the many other English weights that show this ridge. Ray Annenberg described how this button was made. After the canes were set-up in a cast iron or steel ring, they were picked up by a small gather of glass on the end of the pontil rod and worked until smooth. Then a second worker, with a larger gather of glass, gently allows this to fall slowly onto the button being held by the first worker. After cutting off the required amount, the first worker continued to smooth and shape the weight. This method of gently pressing glass onto the button ensures that the ridge mark has a rounded edge. The pontil mark is almost always removed by grinding.

Spiral Paperweights. Height 3.5". Dia. 3". $75-100 Each. ***Author's Collection.***

Two paperweights made by Whitefriars in the 1950-60s. Made in unlimited quantities for the gift trades, these pieces are extremely well made with a great deal of care and attention. The bubble and spiral designs are fascinating to view and these were my first purchase on the paperweight trail.

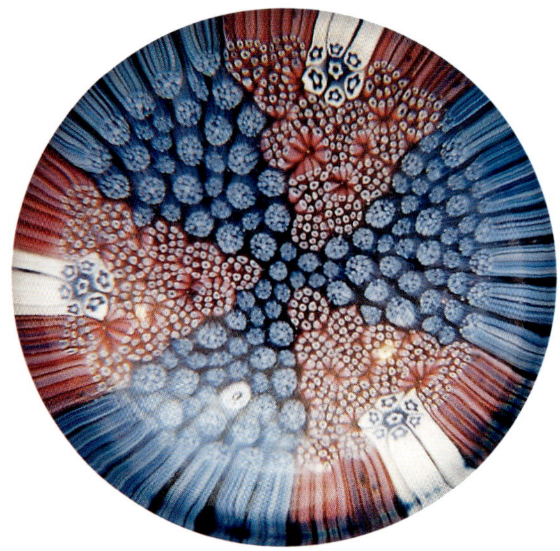

Paneled Paperweight. Height 1.9". Dia. 2.75". $450-550. ***Courtesy of the Stone Gallery, Burford, England.***

Whitefriars paperweights show that the designers tried many antique and modern designs. The panel paperweight was perfected in the mid nineteenth century by Saint Louis, whose panel and tricolor weights fetch many thousands of dollars at auction.

Inkwell Dated 1977. Height 5.5". $750-1000. ***Courtesy of Terry and Hilary Johnson.***

The inkwells produced by Whitefriars are much prized by collectors worldwide, although they were made in quite small limited editions of twenty-five or fifty. If a piece sold well, then they repeated the inkwell with small variations to the design work. This inkwell is limited to fifty pieces but I have seen an almost identical inkwell that was limited to twenty-five pieces which was also a commemorative piece for Queen Elizabeth's Silver Jubilee. This was a practice that explains the quite subtle differences that are found in almost identical limited editions.

Comemorative Paperweight, 1977. Height 2". Dia. 3.25". $300-400. ***Courtesy of The Stone Gallery, Burford, England.***

This paperweight was one version of the Silver Jubilee weight brought out in 1977; although produced in large numbers, it proved to be so successful that another version was created that also sold well.

Butterfly Weight, Dated 1980. Height 1.9". Dia. 3.1". $700-850. ***Author's Collection.***

Whitefriars created these mosaic pictures in the centres of paperweights, produced from 1975 until the factory closed in 1980 by bundling together hundreds of small rods and securing them in moulds ready to be picked up on the button. The rods in this butterfly total in excess of one hundred and thirty. The centre is surrounded by five concentric rows of precisely set, star canes.

Millefiori Ashtray. Dia. 4". $100-150. ***Author's Collection.***

Glass everyday items were also made by Whitefriars, including decanters and dishes, but very few were made and are quite rare objects. Decanters were made with millefiori stoppers and occasionally with canes in the base as well.

Robin Weight, Dated 1977. Height 1.9". Dia. 3". $600-750. ***Author's Collection.***

Many of the picture weights are faceted on five or six sides with a window on top. The workers who set the canes into moulds were usually women, who were more dexterous than the men. The canes were placed with tweezers and an infinite amount of care. The canes in the robin total over two hundred individual rods of varying color shades. The finished mosaic was then covered with a layer of thick white glass. This is usually done by pushing and working a gather of molten white glass down and over the mosaic cane, as you would pull on a glove.

1979 Owl Weight. Height 2". Dia. 3.1". $750-1000. ***Author's Collection.***

This is one of the most sought-after Whitefriars weights. Made in a small, unknown limited edition, the owl is made from bundles of complex canes and surrounded by yellow stars. The whole set-up is garlanded with a row of complex canes, which all sit on a dark blue ground. Five and one faceting enhances the weight to perfection. This is possibly the pinnacle of Whitefriars paperweight production with the artistic set-up of the canes and design. This weight is as good as it gets.

1980 Olympic Weight. Height 2". Dia. 3.3". $350-450. ***Author's Collection.***

A paperweight designed to celebrate the 1980 Olympics in Moscow, which were held despite several nations boycotting them for political reasons. The five circles of interlinked canes, symbolizing the five continents, have the Olympic torch and date set above. The button has been flashed in a light blue glass; the final dome is in clear glass. Six and one facets complete a beautiful paperweight.

1978 Spaced Millefiori. Height 2". Dia. 3.1". $450-550.
Authors Collection.

A carpet of flower-like canes all set on a green flashed ground make this a very pretty weight. The canes are well constructed and complex, with up to fifty rods in a single flower head. Designed to resemble a meadow of wild flowers, the yellow, pink, blue, lilac, and white complex canes are placed at random with great effect. This weight is numbered five but with no indication to edition size.

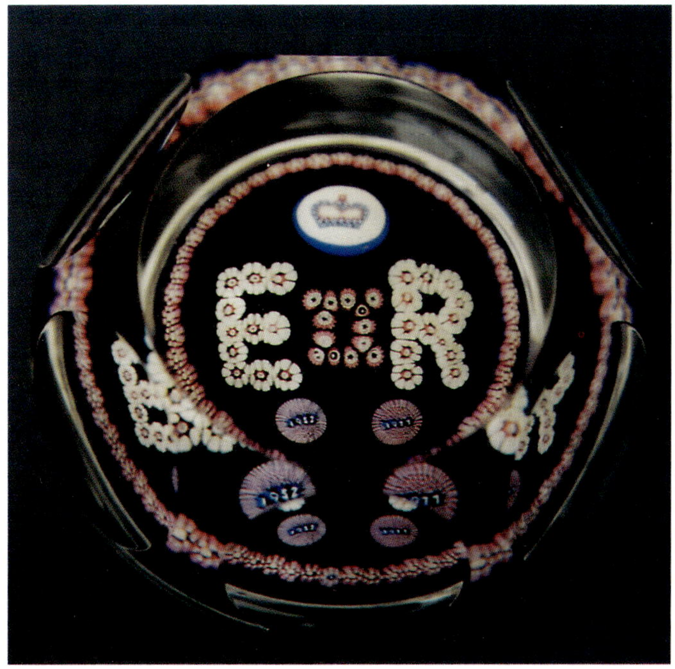

Silver Jubilee Paperweight. Height 2.1". Dia. 3". $400-450. ***Author's Collection.***

This dated 1952-77 commemorative weight is set on a dark blue background, and faceted with six sides and one window on the top. The motif is garlanded with pink and white complex cog canes.

1977 Five Row Concentric. Height 2.1". Dia. 3". $300-400. ***Author's Collection.***

A strikingly colored concentric made from dark blue, and yellow with white encased stars and cog canes. All simply arranged around a central larger star cane. In all of the best quality and limited editions from Whitefriars, you will find the Whitefriars symbol of a white hooded monk in a complex cane with the date included.

Interlinked Garland Jubilee Paperweight. Height 2.1". Dia. 3". $400-500 *Author's Collection.*

Two shades of pink canes make this a spectacular garland weight. Using only simple cog canes, the weight is set upon a dark blue ground to great effect, all set around a crown on a white background.

Six Row Concentric. Height 2.1". Dia. 3". $400-450. *Author's Collection.*

Deep faceting all over with a window on top was a Whitefriars specialty. Dated 1979 with an unknown edition size. A lovely weight to hold and a tribute to the cutters at Whitefriars.

Close Pack Millefiori. Height 2.1". Dia. 3.1". $250-350. *Author's Collection.*

This is an unlimited edition without the Whitefriars logo or date included. This cheaper type of weight can also be found in various colors and faceted. This may be an early predecessor to the quality pieces made in the 1970s until the firm closed down in 1980.

Whitefriars 1977 Decanter and 1973 Inkwell. Decanter: Height 10.25". Inkwell: Height 5.6". ***Photo, Courtesy of L.H. Selman Ltd.***

The stopper on this decanter has an arrangement of complex cog, star, and floret canes in pistachio green, brown, and white. The stopper has been cut with five and one facets. The bottle is decorated with elongated oval facets, and the main body has a diamond-trellis cut with a star cut base. This piece was purchased by the author in the 1997 Fall auction of L.H. Selman Ltd. for $620. The inkwell-perfume bottle was in the same auction and realized $800. The inkwell went to an unknown buyer. The five rows of complex cog and star canes in pink, white, and blue appear in the base and stopper. A date and signature shows on a single cane.

Whitefriars Christmas Paperweight. Height 2.5". Dia. 3". $500-600. ***Courtesy of Marion Langham.***

This Christmas weight is part of a limited edition of five hundred, but the Whitefriars records held by Caithness Glass, who bought the company in receivership, show that most limited editions were never produced in full. In many cases an edition of one thousand may have resulted in only three or four hundred being produced. A five hundred edition may result in as little as one hundred paperweights produced. This would explain the rarity of some editions.

Blue and White Flower Garland. Height 2.5". Dia. 3". $350-400. ***Author's Collection.***

This weight was made by Caithness Glass of Scotland, after the company had bought the name Whitefriars from the receivers in 1980. Caithness has continued to use the Hooded Monk logo, made famous by James Powell and Whitefriars, in their production of paperweights made in recent years. They have continued a tradition of fine collector's weights which are now sold worldwide. These weights, of collector quality, are limited editions and numbered. Some of the bases are star cut, an attractive addition that Whitefriars never used on any of their weights.

Alpine Pinks. Height 2.5". Dia. 3". $350-400. *Author's Collection.*

Another example of a Caithness Whitefriars paperweight. Signed on the base Caithness Whitefriars in a limited edition of two hundred and fifty and with a White Monk cane included in the garland.

Whitefriars Color Catalogue 1980, Inside Pages.

This was the best and last catalogue produced by Whitefriars. Their last major trade fair at the National Exhibition Centre, Birmingham, in 1980 did not produce enough orders from the gift trade to carry the factory for another year, so the receivers were called in to liquidate the company. I attended this last trade exhibition personally and visited the Whitefriars stand, where I bought a large cut glass vase. Although Whitefriars only took orders at trade shows, it was common practice to sell off display stock at the end of a show. Shortly after this show, I was visited by a former worker for the company at my business premises where he explained that the company was now finished and would I like to buy samples of their weights as he knew I collected paperweights. The price he asked for each and every weight was $30. As I already had twelve or more in my collection I declined his offer, a decision that still haunts me even now; with hindsight we could all be wealthy people.

Millefiore paperweights

Beautiful colours and patterns have always held a fascination for mankind. Millefiore paperweights are especially elegant individual creations, each bed of colourful and decorative canes being encapsulated in a dome of highest quality English full lead crystal.

The earliest known dated Whitefriars paperweight was made in 1848. Over one hundred years later a millefiore paperweight is today just as skilfully and carefully hand crafted by dedicated masters of the glassmaking trade.

New colours, many based on those developed for use in the stained glass windows produced in the famous Whitefriars studios and introduced into Whitefriars paperweights in more modern times have served to increase public interest in millefiore paperweights.

Ancient processes have more recently been blended with modern technical developments to extend the variety of patterns into new areas. Paperweights are made entirely by hand, from the initial melting of a wide range of special colours, the creation of glass cane, the complete hand setting of the patterns, the hand making by traditional craft methods, to the completion of the paperweight by hand cutting or faceting, all within Whitefriars factory.

Whitefriars introduced the first of an annual series of Christmas millefiore paperweights in 1975. These paperweights are collectors commemorative limited editions. They, with ink bottles and decanters, are enthusiastically sought after by collectors all over the world.

Development is a continuous process and new Whitefriars millefiore paperweight designs are regularly introduced into the extensive range by the Company's Chief Designer—Geoffrey Baxter Des.R.C.A. M.S.I.A.

Commemorativ

To meet the demand from collectors, Whi
have issued special commemorative limite
for such occasions as the Silver Jubilee of H
Queen Elizabeth II, sailing of the "Mayflo
Bi-centenary of the U.S.A. and the Anniv
the Founding of the State of Israel, as well

A thousand flov

Today every Whitefriars millefiore paperweigh
the insignia and date hidden deep in the "thousa
flowers", as this photograph illustrates.

Since 1680, Whitefriars have designed and
articles in English full lead crystal which h
collected,'treasured and handed down fro
generation to generation.

During that span of time, the master glass
developed their own particular style in the
production of millefiore paperweights.

The word millefiore meaning "a thousand
is Italian in origin although the most form
work was created by the French in the nin
century. Along with the names of such ma
Clichy, St. Louis and Baccarat appears Wh
Today, just as over one hundred years ago

Whitefriars

Tudor Road, Wealdstone, Middlesex HA3

erweights

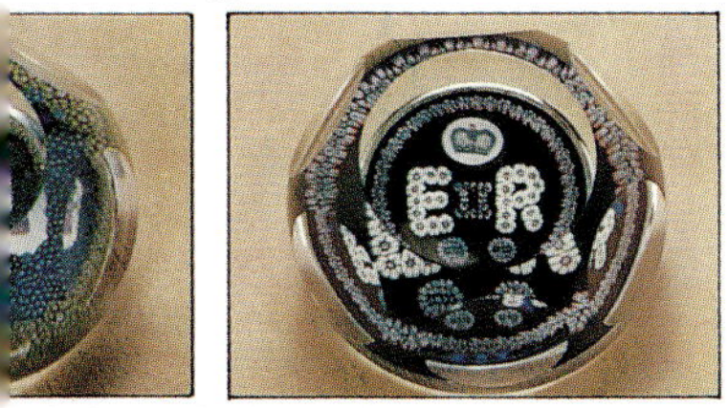

ted editions for the Smithsonian Institution of
erica. A limited edition Christmas paperweight
so produced annually. Every limited edition
commemorative issue is accompanied with a
tificate of Authenticity, and each article is
rly numbered and suitably boxed.

*h paperweight is presented in a satin lined
eet—a mark of the respect given it by the
ismen of Whitefriars.*

lefiore paperweights are made carefully and
ividually by dedicated craftsmen. Every
erweight differs slightly and each one has its
n charm.

lefiore paperweights designed and made at
itefriars are available in a wide variety of styles
colours.

versatility of handsetting each piece of cane in
nfinitely variable pattern, together with the
rnative background colours gives an almost
less choice of designs and colours to delight the
of the paperweight connoisseur.

Limited

Telephone: 01-427 1527/0358 Telex: 929 519

Whitefriars Color Catalogue 1980, Outside Pages.

In the description of millefiori paperweights, Whitefriars themselves state that "the earliest known dated Whitefriars paperweight was made in 1848," but I suspect that this is only hearsay, and that they were referring to Arculus or Walsh-Walsh weights from the 1920-30s that were thought to be Whitefriars.

Cut patterns

Whitefriars

Hand made English full lead crystal
Each paperweight is supplied in its own satin lined Gift Box

P1 (uncut)

P2 Window cut

P3 Diamond cut

P5 Tall dome-finger cut

P9 Window and small mitre cuts

P10 Large facet cut

P11 Brick cut

P14 Miniature window cut

P16 Lace twist window cut

P17 Small brick cut lace twist

P18 Large facets lace twist

P19 Large facets and mitre cuts lace twist

P20 Large brick cuts lace twist

P21 Double window cut lace twist

P25 Setting of miniature paperweights and close set canes, window cut

P26 Window and small ball cuts

P27 Window and mitre cuts

P30 'Pedestal' window cut

P31 Setting of single canes mixed with florette canes, plain

P32 Setting of close packed multihued canes, windowed cut

P33 Window cut top surrounded by close mitre cuts, various settings and backing colours

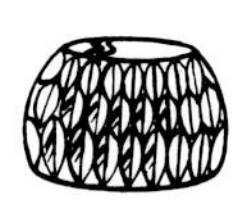
P34 Window cut top surrounded by close mitre cuts, various settings

P35 'Spray' Lace twist canes with florette setting D/B L/B G

P36 'Spray' setting of a variety of florettes D/B L/B G

P37 Miniature lace twist

P38 'Vortex' window cut D/B L/B G

P39 Large pedestal window cut

Alternative ba

Certain millefiore paperw
These are indicated again

Dark Blue Background =
Light Blue Background =
Green Background =

P40 Coloured 'can twist' canes close set in florettes

P41 Coloured 'can twist' and window cut with small window D/B L/B G

PG100 'Garland' classical setting of interwoven cane, plain D/B L/B G

PG101 'Garland' classical setting of interwoven canes D/B L/B G

PG102 'Garland' random setting of many coloured canes, plain D/B L/B G

PG103 'Garland' window cut D/B L/B G

PG104 'Posy' window cut D/B L/B G

PG105 Miniature garland window cut D/B L/B G

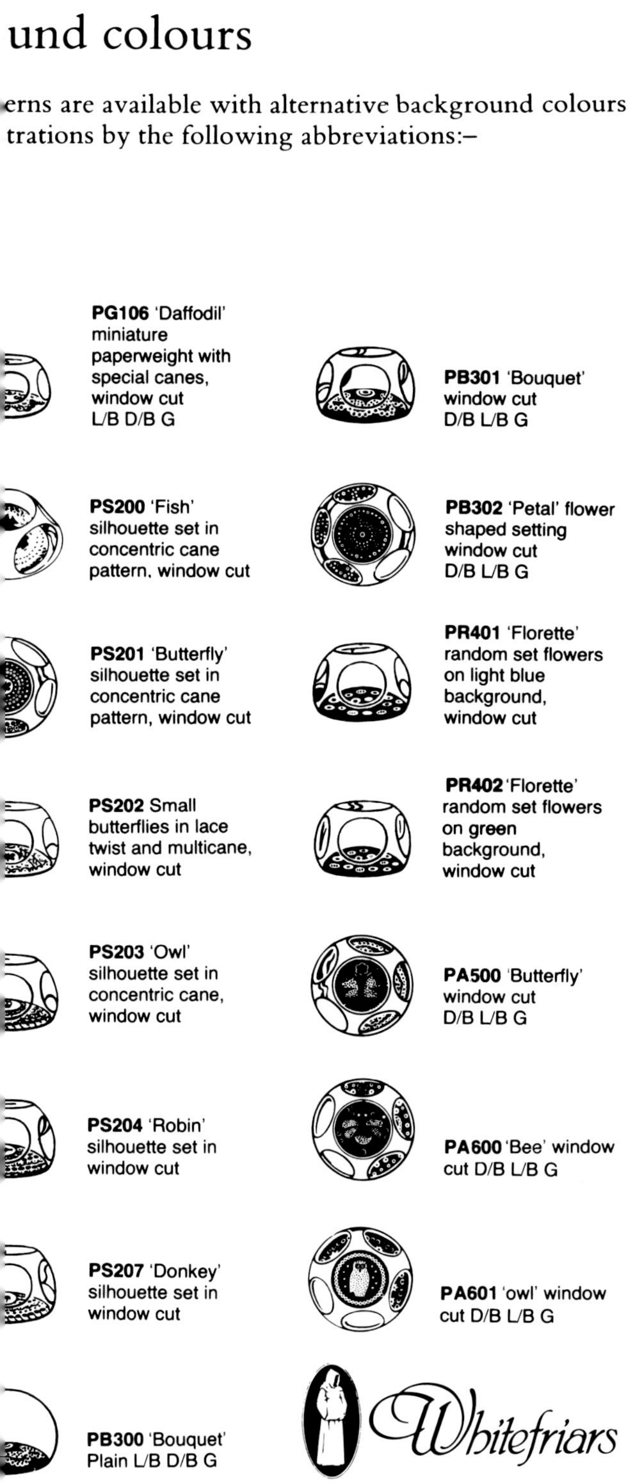

und colours

erns are available with alternative background colours
trations by the following abbreviations:–

PG106 'Daffodil' miniature paperweight with special canes, window cut L/B D/B G

PS200 'Fish' silhouette set in concentric cane pattern, window cut

PS201 'Butterfly' silhouette set in concentric cane pattern, window cut

PS202 Small butterflies in lace twist and multicane, window cut

PS203 'Owl' silhouette set in concentric cane, window cut

PS204 'Robin' silhouette set in window cut

PS207 'Donkey' silhouette set in window cut

PB300 'Bouquet' Plain L/B D/B G

PB301 'Bouquet' window cut D/B L/B G

PB302 'Petal' flower shaped setting window cut D/B L/B G

PR401 'Florette' random set flowers on light blue background, window cut

PR402 'Florette' random set flowers on green background, window cut

PA500 'Butterfly' window cut D/B L/B G

PA600 'Bee' window cut D/B L/B G

PA601 'owl' window cut D/B L/B G

Whitefriars

Whitefriars Black and White Catalogue, c. 1980.

This catalogue gives most of the production range, with the numerous variations that could be ordered by a trade buyer at an exhibition.

Millefiore Decanters, Dishes and Ink Bottles.

CM637 cut crystal Square Spirit Decanter with Millefiore stopper

CM625 Decanter with Millefiore stopper. Hand cut crystal

9754 Millefiore Bottle 5¼″ high Gift Boxed

Although paperweights are the items which most usually incorporate millefiore patterns, a wide variety of other items were also produced during the nineteenth century using this highly decorative technique. One of the earliest pieces dated 1848 was a Whitefriars ink bottle – a reproduction of this bottle is still made for today's collector and is produced by hand methods identical to those originally used. Hand cut full lead crystal decanters individually fitted with decorative millefiore stoppers and plain cut crystal dishes with millefiore centres are also produced and make delightfully decorative gifts.

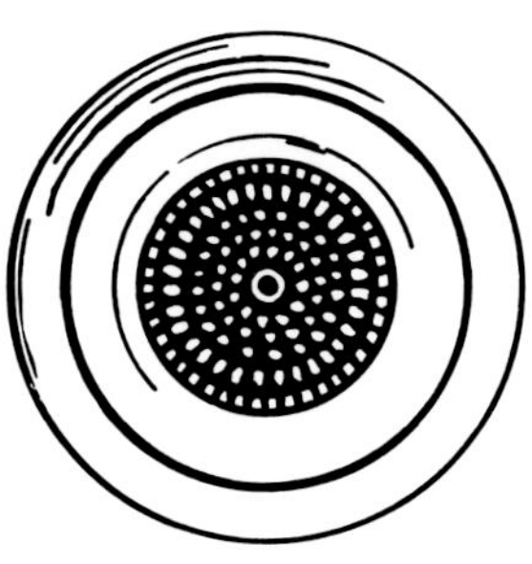

9739 Millefiore dish, plain uncut 4½″ diam. colour and pattern various (boxed)

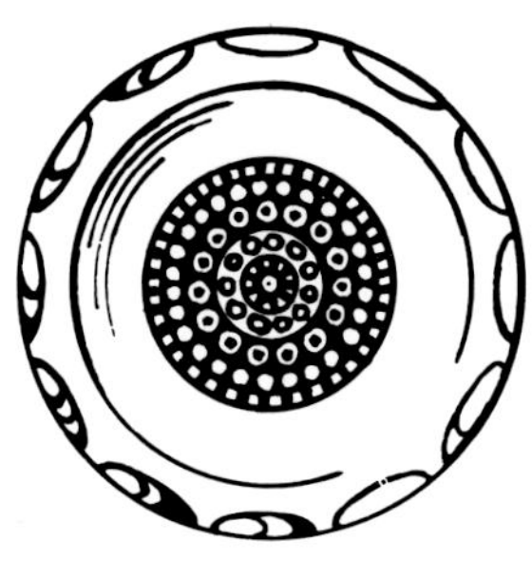

9755 Millefiore dish, cut crystal 4½″ diam. colours and patterns various

9756 Millefiore dish, cut crystal 4½″ diam.

Settings

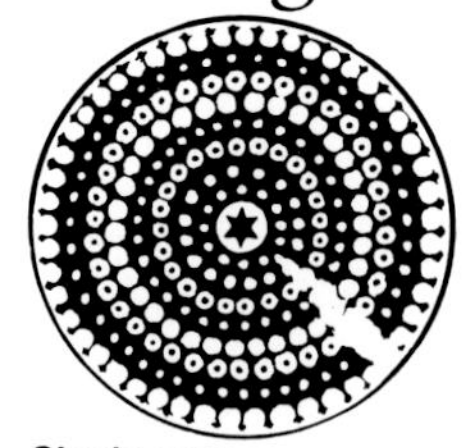

Single cane
set in concentric rings

'Spray'
P36 Cane pattern
P35 Lace Twist & Cane

P25 **Cane bunches**
set within florettes

Whitefriars millefiore pap
incorporates a cane conta
assembled individually b
combinations.

Whitefri

Tudor Road, Wealdstone

Whitefriars Black and White Trade Catalogue, c. 1980.

Whitefriars again mention that "one of the earliest pieces dated 1848 was a Whitefriars inkbottle- a reproduction of this bottle is still made for today's collector..."A company with the reputation of Whitefriars would surely not try to mislead the collecting public but were themselves misled. As were we all until the existence of Arculus and Walsh-Walsh became known, and the fact that they made dated weights and inkwells from c. 1920.

Chapter Thirteen

Unknown Makers

A chapter on English, unattributable paperweights could be a book in its own right. The problem with trying to allocate a paperweight to a particular glassworks is immense, mainly because these "trinkets in glass" were usually only produced as a side line, and so virtually no records were kept. In the 1850s, Birmingham had no fewer than sixty glassworks in operation. Some of these were small works with just several employees, and it is reasonable to assume that at some time during the life of these tiny glasshouses, the workers tried their hands at paperweights. This would account for the tremendous variety of styles and quality that can be seen on the following pages. It is quite probable that many of these older unknown pieces will eventually find their correct place in the historical evolution of the English paperweight, but for the time being they must be relegated to the back pages of this book. Their placement on the back pages does not necessarily mean these items are of no consequence or beauty. On the contrary, some of these paperweights are extremely beautiful and very important, but unfortunately I cannot find a link to a glassworks that could identify them with a reasonable degree of certainty. However I am sure that will not be the case for too long.

Blue and White Overlayed Six Row Concentric. Dia. 2.8". $1250-1500. ***Collection of Karen & Paul Dunlop, © 1997 Papier Presse.***

A very unusual faceted overlay weight. The only clue to its identification could be in the five rows of canes that have crosses as centres. A concentric in the Bacchus section also has five rows of crosses of a very similar shape. Bacchus were known to have made overlays and crosses, and have faceted their weights.

Unknown Concentric. Dia. 2.2". $1000-1250. ***Collection of Karen & Paul Dunlop, © 1997 Papier Presse.***

A very beautiful five row concentric using mainly white canes to give it a carpet ground appearance. The four spaced outer canes in red and white plus blue and white give the weight an extra appeal. The central cane is well made and a good focal point. A very desirable paperweight.

Four Row Concentric. Dia. 3.2". $1250-1500. *Collection of Karen & Paul Dunlop © 1997 Papier Presse.*

A stunning weight with a fine variety of well-made complex canes; the pink ruffles have a definite Bacchus look. All set around a lovely central ruffle.

Close Packed Concentric. Dia 3.7". $1000-1250. *Collection of Karen & Paul Dunlop, © 1997 Papier Presse.*

This magnum paperweight contains a large central cane with a thick cross that looks similar to a Bacchus cruciform cane. The weight is large enough and has the same flared set-up of canes that many Bacchus paperweights have; it is indeed beautiful enough to be from Bacchus with its soft pastel colors and delicate canes.

Six Row Concentric with Thirty-Seven Silhouettes of Queen Victoria. Dia. 2.8". $1500-2000. ***Collection of Karen & Paul Dunlop, © 1997 Papier Presse.***

A rare example by an unknown maker. The row of thirty-seven heads makes this piece almost unique; one other example exists in a private collection with the same row of Victoria Heads. The other rows of canes are tightly packed and well constructed. A similar piece can also be seen in this chapter with nine Victoria Heads.

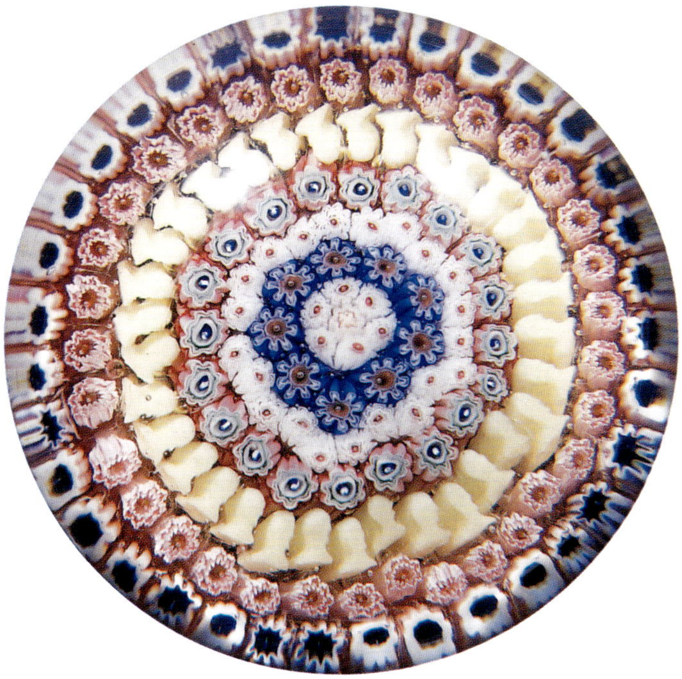

Seven Row Concentric with Thirty-Three Silhouettes of Prince Albert. Dia. 3.25". $1500-2000. *Collection of Karen & Paul Dunlop, © 1997 Papier Presse.*

This paperweight is possibly unique, in that this is the first paperweight the Author has seen or heard about with a row of Prince Albert heads. This weight is almost certainly from the same maker as the weight with the thirty-seven Victoria Heads. Both are superb examples of quality English workmanship.

Three Row Concentric. Height 2.25". Dia. 2.75". *Courtesy of Terry and Hilary Johnson.*

The canes in this weight are drawn down and under the base to where the pontil is broken off and unground. The canes were all cut to the same length to leave the base tidily finished off.

Six Row Concentric Magnum. Height 2.5". Dia. 4". $500-750. *Courtesy of Terry and Hilary Johnson.*

A magnum size paperweight mainly of simply constructed cog canes. The weight has a rough pontil and sits on an inverted foot.

Profile of Three Row Concentric.

This footed paperweight shows a large dome of glass for a relatively small set-up of canes.

Five Row Magnum Concentric with Victoria Head Cane. Height 2.2". Dia. 4.1". $1000-1500. ***Courtesy of Anne Anderson***

A remarkable paperweight with the first ever bottle green head cane. The head does not conform to the easily recognized Victoria Silhouettes we see in Bacchus weights; this head is softer in profile and fuller in the face. Could this be an attempt to portray the older Queen Victoria?

Profile of Concentric with Green Head Cane.

The profile shows a low dome shape with steeply falling sides. The base has a rough pontil with the canes cut to a precise length, the same as a Richardson paperweight.

Close-up of Concentric with Green Head Cane.

This close-up shows the head cane low down near the base. The next row has white cross canes in a deep blue ground but the canes in the next row are superb complex canes. These canes are red and white pastry moulds with a combination of canes as its centre. Whoever made this paperweight put in enough appeal to keep the observer interested.

Five Row Concentric. Height 1.75". Dia. 2.7". $400-500. *Private Collection.*

This paperweight has the canes set up like a bouquet. The rounded tuft has the outside row of canes drawn down and under to the centre of the base. The five rows of pink and white canes are set around a large blue cog with a red centre.

Base of Five Row Concentric.

The pontil is left unground with the base slightly concave, and with a large, almost flat, basal ring.

Close Packed Concentric. Height 2.2". Dia. 3.5". $350-400. *Courtesy of Anne Anderson.*

This strikingly colored paperweight has simple but bright canes set around a large red flower head. The base is slightly concave with a ridge mark where the two halves were joined together, and has a rough pontil mark.

Four Row Concentric with Twenty-one Heads. Height 1.75". Dia. 2.75". $750-1000. *Private Collection.*

A complete row of twenty-one Victoria Heads can be seen in the second row from the outside in this paperweight. The maker has used pale blues and whites around a central red and blue cane. The placement of canes is rather untidy; the head canes are placed in all directions which leaves the viewer confused. The base shows a slightly ground, concave base with untidy, uneven ends.

Five Row Concentric. Height 2.5". Dia. 3.3". $300-350. *Author's Collection.*

The high dome makes this paperweight a little different from the rest. The strongly colored simple canes, drawn untidily beneath the weight to the rough pontil, possibly points to a Walsh-Walsh attribution.

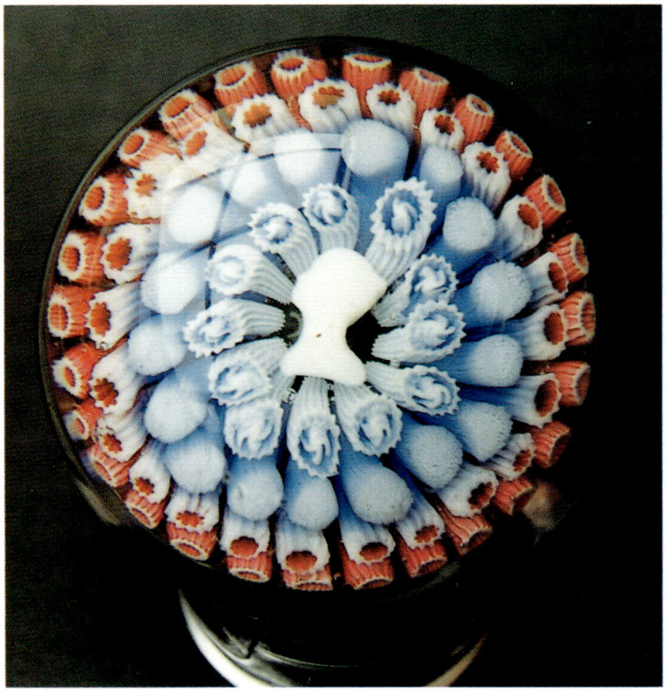

Four Row Concentric with Victoria Head. Height 1.6". Dia. 3.25". $750-1000. ***Courtesy of Terry and Hilary Johnson.***

A striking silhouette sits as the central cane in this weight. Not only is there a lovely head, but also a remarkable cane that is so closely packed with tiny cog canes, ninety-eight in total, that it looks almost solid. It contains the most rods in a complex cane I have ever seen. The white head in clear glass is very well made and deserves its central position.

Candle Holder with Millefiori Cushion. Height 2.2". Dia. 2". $150-200. ***Author's Collection.***

A very pretty object, neatly made with strongly colored canes and faceted all over. This item was bought in the Birmingham area and was possibly made in Birmingham originally. Badly damaged when first acquired. It has been refaceted to remove the damaged sharp edges.

Base of Silhouette weight.

In this paperweight the outer row of canes have been drawn beneath the weight to the centre; the pontil has been broken off to leave it rough. A ridge can be seen where the two halves were joined together. The profile shows a low dome and is similar to the low dome paperweights from the Arculus/Walsh-Walsh factories, but so far I have not come across any weights from these two factories with canes such as the ones displayed in this lovely example. The cane ends are left looking like the Bacchus examples to be found in this book, drawn towards the centre and neatly finished.

Base of Candle Holder.

The base shows the cane ends all cut to the same lengths. The cane cushion and base have been finished off by applying heat to the bottom of the piece, smoothing out the pontil and rough edges.

Pansy Weight, Unknown Maker. Height 2". Dia. 2.5". $400-500.
Courtesy of Margaret Preston.

This pansy weight has a patriotic Victorian look. The Union Flag can be seen on the petals of this symbolic Victorian flower, a favourite subject for paperweight makers of the past and present. The base has a flat rough pontil.

Five Row Pink and Blue Concentric, Height 2". Dia. 3.6". $500-700
Author's Collection.

A large concentric from the Birmingham area, bought at auction with the following two paperweights from the same collection. These three pieces have the same dimensions of many of the Arculus and Walsh-Walsh paperweights, and it is possible that this could be of their origin. However, these paperweights have the bases finished off, neat and tidy, similar to the Bacchus and French way of drawing the canes beneath the base and leaving a spoke effect. This finishing process to the bases demonstrates a degree of skill and quality that is sadly lacking in many early twentieth century paperweights. Unlike Bacchus and the French manufacturers, the glassmaker who made these paperweights left the pontils rough. All the bases are concave with a slight ridge to be felt where the two halves were joined together. Several of the canes are quite complex with crosses featured in all of the three weights. All three also have large central feature canes that are well made and deserve to be the centre focal point. The cane cushions are set low in the bases, relying on the magnifying power of the glass to fill out the weight.

Close Pack, Unknown Maker. Height 2.25". Dia. 3.2". $200-300.
Courtesy of Mr. & Mrs. Richard Giles.

This close pack is filled with simple cogs and tubes covered in clear glass to give the impression of space between the canes.

Base of Five Row Pink and Blue Concentric.

Four Row Concentric. Height 1.8". Dia. 3.75". $500-600. *Author's Collection.*

This paperweight shows distinctive cross canes which I have been unable to match to any known examples. The red and green cane in the second row from the centre looks very similar to the Walsh-Walsh canes held at the Broadfield House Glass Museum. In this row can also be seen a "rogue" cane. This cane is not a slipped cane and has been deliberately placed in this row. This method of a worker identifying a piece was practiced by the nineteenth century glassworkers of Bacchus. It is just possible that an apprentice aged thirteen or fourteen years, beginning work in the 1860s, could still be working in the glass industry in the early part of the twentieth century, when we know paperweights were being made by the Arculus and Walsh-Walsh companies. This type of paperweight shows several signs of the Bacchus techniques, such as the flaring out of the canes and the use of a large central cane so popular with Bacchus. The canes are drawn down and under to make a basket that finishes the base of the weight so precisely, and, as in similar Bacchus examples, use pastel shades. Without any doubt, workers moved around in the glass business as employees do today and the same applies to the ownership of glasshouses. Almost all glasshouses in the nineteenth and twentieth centuries changed hands on numerous occasions. Each owner of a newly acquired business knows that the most precious item acquired is the skilled workforce that comes with it. Unless a newly acquired business was bought for its assets or the company's secrets, the workforce would have been passed on like a favourite heirloom. The techniques and skills would also have been passed on through the years. The tradition in families for sons to follow in their father's footsteps was also very strong at this period in time. The French glasshouse of Baccarat is a prime example of this traditional father to son passing on of the skills acquired and secretly guarded. Baccarat today still provides houses for skilled workers, which have been lived in by the family and passed on to sons, who have carried on the family loyalty to their employer. These houses are set in a square around the entrance to the glasshouse. Traditionally, a bell was rung when the glass is at the correct temperature for working; workers would stop whatever they were doing and report for work immediately. This was probably true of other English makers as well. Bacchus and the Islington glasshouses were in the centre of the Birmingham industrial areas with the factories all having rows of small terraced houses attached or close to the factories, close enough to call in workers when the glass was ready to work.

Base of Four Row Concentric.

The spokes can be seen to great effect here. The outside canes are drawn under with the ridge mark and broken pontil visible.

Five Row Blue and Red Concentric, Unknown Maker. Height 2". Dia. 3.5". $500-600. *Author's Collection.*

This paperweight is precisely set in well-spaced concentric rows. Simple cross and cog canes surround the large central ribbed cog cane with a blue cross centre.

Four Row Concentric, Unknown Maker. Height 2". Dia. 3.3". $350-450. *Author's Collection.*

This paperweight is constructed in the same way as in the three previous examples. Tubes and solid canes surround a central large cog cane. The outer row of solid red cogs are drawn beneath the weight to the centre of the base, creating a spoke effect.

Five Row Concentric. Height 2.6". Dia. 3.5". $300-400. *Courtesy of Mr. and Mrs. Richard Giles.*

This very simple paperweight is neatly presented and may have been made to be part of an inkwell. An almost identical inkwell base is known.

Base of Five Row Blue and Red Concentric.

The base of this paperweight is the equal of many Bacchus paperweights. The precise way the canes have been drawn down and finished off is surely a sign of skills inherited, directly or indirectly, from the Bacchus workers in the classic period of the 1850s. It is possible that we shall never know the identity of the paperweight maker who made this piece, or even the glasshouse it came from, but I take my hat off to the worker who made these pieces in the style of the Bacchus concentrics. When the popularity of the paperweight began to decline in the latter part of the nineteenth century, many of the skills needed for this process began to be lost. These few paperweights show signs of the earlier skills, and were possibly an attempt to revive the market.

Base of Five Row Concentric.

The base of this weight is prettier than the crown. The canes on the outside edge look as though they were placed just for the purpose of completing the base tidily.

Four Row Concentric. Height 2.1". Dia. 3.6". $250-300. *Author's Collection.*

Pale pinks and white make up this simple paperweight. A rather plain and uninteresting example from an unknown maker.

Four Row Concentric. Height 2.4". Dia. 3.3". $350-450. *Author's Collection.*

This weight has an interesting row of canes surrounding the central white star. This cane is composed of twelve small tubes and rods and encased in a cog cane, all in pale pinks and whites. The other solid canes, although simply made, make this an attractive paperweight.

Five Row Concentric. Height 1.75". Dia. 3.25". $300-400. *Author's Collection.*

Thick cross canes in green and white can be found in this poorly made paperweight. I suspect that this piece could be from the Arculus glasshouse. Little thought has gone into the cane set-up, with odd canes appearing all over the weight.

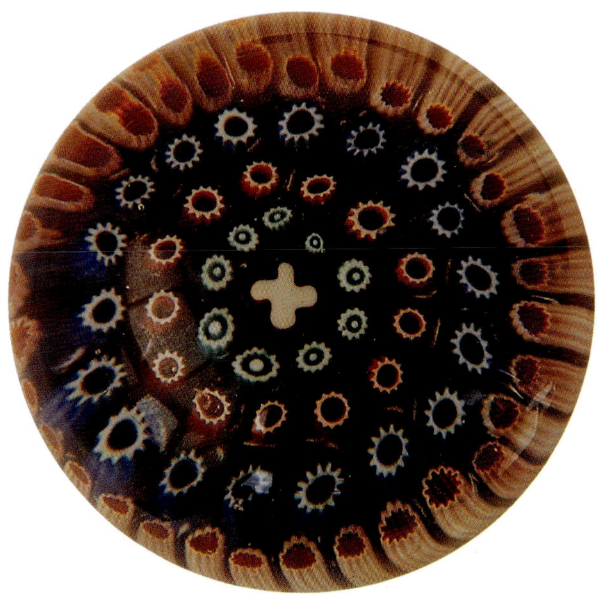

Four Row Concentric. Height 2.4". Dia. 3.6". $300-400. *Author's Collection.*

A high dome concentric with a white cross as a centre. The tube and cog canes are surrounded by a row of red and white tubes which are drawn under the base to the centre. The base is almost flat with the pontil lightly ground off. There is no ridge mark and the cane set-up reaches almost to the base, rising only the length of the canes into the crown, approximately 1/2".

Inkwell Base. Height 1.5". Dia. 3.5". $200-300. *Author's Collection.*

This inkwell base was salvaged from the scrap bin by cutting the bulbous body down in size to make this paperweight. The inkwell was found in badly damaged condition with no alternative but regrinding. The canes are offset in the base but were hardly noticeable with the body of the inkwell still in place. The piece is footed, with the canes drawn to the centre of the concave base. The rough pontil has been left in place. The canes are simple cogs and tubes around the large cog centre which was not quite compatible with the rest of the glass in the weight, as annealing cracks surround the cane, appearing as silver reflections.

Five Row Concentric. Height 1.6". Dia. 3.1". $200-300. *Author's Collection.*

Tightly packed, better than average canes packed around a well made cog and star centre, from an unknown maker, make this paperweight a little more interesting. The maker tried to draw the outside row of pale lilac and white canes to the centre of the base. He succeeded in creating a nice basket effect but left a broken pontil mark in excess of 1" to obscure and spoil the whole effect.

Five Row Concentric. Height 3.5". Dia. 3.4". $250-350. *Author's Collection.*

Solid cogs and a row of tubes make up this concentric. The outer row of solid white cogs are drawn beneath the weight to the centre and lightly ground to remove the pontil mark. This weight has steep sides and a flat base. There is a slight ridge to be felt where the two halves of the paperweight have been joined together. This and the previous paperweight were probably made by the same unknown glassworks.

Spaced Concentric. Height 2.75". Dia. 3.5". *Courtesy of Mr. & Mrs. Richard Giles.*

This paperweight has the right dimensions to be an early Bacchus, and if canes could be matched with known pieces, then this weight becomes very valuable. A price of $750-1000 would be appropriate for a weight that has canes which are not of the highest quality. If this is a Bacchus weight, then it must be an early piece as the quality of Bacchus weights are usually of the highest order. The outside canes are drawn to the base centre to leave a rough pontil.

Five Row Concentric. Height 2.6". Dia. 3.25". $450-550. *Courtesy of Mr. & Mrs. Richard Giles.*

The outside row of white canes has collected a little dirt and grit from the mould that holds the canes, prior to picking up with the first gather of molten glass. The paperweight has a preciseness about it that may link it to the Richardson glasshouse of Stourbridge.

Base of Five Row Concentric.

The canes are finished in the base centre with a slight twist. This spoke effect is a quality finish to the base, and adds to the attractiveness of the weight. Unfortunately, a large broken pontil has been left, when a slight touch on the grinding wheel would have made all the difference.

Close Pack. Height 2.25". Dia. 3.2". $350-450. Courtesy of *Mr. & Mrs. Richard Giles.*

An attractive close pack with all the canes encased in clear glass to give the weight an open look to it. The central red and blue cane is of a good quality, with the rest being cogs, solid, and tube canes of various colors. The outside canes are drawn to the centre with the pontil ground off.

Four Row Concentric. Height 2.25". Dia. 3.25". $450-550. *Courtesy of Mr. & Mrs. Richard Giles.*

A large star centre with tubes and solid cogs dipped in a thin color coating make this a desirable weight. The weight is finished beautifully with the outside row drawn to the base centre and ground concavely. This spoke effect on the base makes all the difference, and adds value to the paperweight.

Four Row Concentric. Height 3". Dia. 1.8". $1250-1500. ***Courtesy of Colin McCallien.***

A striking concentric with the white outside canes being large and set in tubes. This method of encasing ruffles and cogs with an outer layer of clear glass, and then a thick tube of white glass to finish, was a favoured method of Bacchus. The large central ruffle in a tube is surrounded by small red and white tubes which were also used by Bacchus. On the basis of the cane likeness to recognized Bacchus canes, this weight should probably be in the Bacchus chapter, but the outer row of brown, almost clear canes that are drawn beneath the weight make this paperweight slightly different. The brown canes are so thinly made that they begin to become feathery as they become elongated towards the centre, unlike the positive and normally solid Bacchus canes. This weight makes the point that paperweight makers were always trying new canes, styles, and other variations. As with the French well-documented paperweights from the classic period of c. 1850, there will always be some that look like, but do not completely conform to, the accepted normal size and shape.

Five Row Concentric. Height 2.1". Dia. 2.9". ***Courtesy of the Private Collection of Anne Metcalfe, The Sweetbriar Gallery, Helsby, England.***

Open ruffle canes with stars and colored tubes all centred on a large red and blue open ruffle cane. The whole weight is well made and presented with the motif perfectly placed in the centre of the weight.

Magnum Door Handle or Newel Post with Silhouettes. Height 3.75" (including mount). Dia. 3.75". $750-1000. ***Author's Collection.***

This is the first English piece I have ever seen mounted on a brass stand. It would be possible to use it as a door handle or newel post top, or even as an ornamental table or mantel piece. The central pastry mould cane has a row of nine white Victoria Heads set in clear glass surrounding it. Many of the canes are untidily set with slippage in all the rows. There are also two rows of red on white cross canes in this very unusual piece. The paperweight part shows the low placed cane set-up covered in a low profile dome of glass. A slight joining mark can be felt beneath the weight with the outside row of canes drawn rather untidily towards the centre of the base. This weight has the untidy look of the Arculus weights from the 1920s about it. When Alfred Arculus and Joseph Warry took over the firm of R.W. Winfield in 1875, the company they bought were manufacturers of Flint glass as a sideline to the main business of Brassfounders. It was only after the take-over that Arculus and Warry concentrated their efforts on glass products only. This may be an important transitional piece which makes the paperweight link back to the 1870s. Is it possible that the paperweights found with head canes were made by Winfields and carried on by Arculus into the early twentieth century? Possibly so, but it is also likely that other manufacturers made silhouette heads from the mid nineteenth century, as illustrated by the variety of colors and styles in this book.

Six Row Concentric. Height 2". Dia. 3.2". *Courtesy of the Private Collection of Anne Metcalfe, The Sweetbriar Gallery, Helsby, England.*

A row of ruffle canes in the style of Bacchus gives this weight plenty of interest. All the canes are better than average, and all show effort and thought in the cane make-up. The cross canes are particularly nice, as they are enclosed in several coats of lacy thin white glass to make up the ruffle. This ruffle cane was extensively used by Bacchus in the 1850s.

Close Packed Millefiori. Height 2". Dia. 2.75". *Courtesy of the Private Collection of Anne Metcalfe, The Sweetbriar Gallery, Helsby, England.*

A whole variety of Bacchus look-alike canes, crosses encased in tubes of white glass, a favourite cane used by Bacchus. This weight has all the attributes to be a Bacchus except for its size and the fact that the canes are not drawn to the centre as with the known Bacchus weights. This may well have been an apprentice piece to use up unwanted odd canes at the end of the day. All glassworkers had to start somewhere on the long road to becoming an expert paperweight maker, and this is probably an early attempt. This is still a very collectible and interesting piece.

Four Row Concentric. Height 2". Dia. 3". *Courtesy of the Private Collection of Anne Metcalfe, The Sweetbriar Gallery, Helsby, England.*

A very pretty weight in cane combinations of pink, white, blue, and green, all set around a blue and white large cog cane. Although this weight is of only of a simple nature, it is interesting to note the type of weights the paperweight dealers collect. With many hundreds of antique and modern paperweights passing through her hands every year, it is notable that Anne, although not a true collector of paperweights, has retained for her own interest several unknowns and 1930s Chinese painted paperweights.

Paperweight with Screw Fitting. Height 2.7". Dia. 3.35". $300-500. *Courtesy of The Sweetbriar Gallery, Helsby, England. (Archive Photo)*

A very unusual millefiori piece with a long screw attachment embedded in the base of the glass. This could be used as a Newel post top or maybe a door handle. The canes and coloring are reminiscent of the Whitefriars glassworks but the central cane looks like many central feature canes from the Stourbridge area, and may be a frigger.

Selection of Paperweights from Archive Photos. ***Courtesy of The Sweetbriar Gallery, Helsby, England.***

This selection of weights was previously on sale at the Sweetbriar Gallery, from 1990 onwards. Most were thought to originate in the Stourbridge and Birmingham areas. Prices today would be between $250 to 500.

Selection of Paperweights from Archive Photos. ***Courtesy of The Sweetbriar Gallery, Helsby, England.***

Five Row Concentric with Fifteen Silhouettes. Height 2". Dia. 2.75". $750-1000. ***Courtesy of Dr. Geoffrey Dutton.***

This is a stunningly precise paperweight; the Victoria Head Silhouettes are superbly crafted, with fine detailing. This weight is almost certainly from the same glassworks as previous Victoria Silhouette paperweights in this chapter on unknown makers. Several of these cog and cross canes can be found in other paperweights from this group of unknowns. The encased star cane in the centre is a superb example of a centre cane.

Base of Concentric with Fifteen Silhouettes.

The cane set-up is quite small, relying on the magnifying property of the glass dome to fill out the paperweight. The base is concave with a rough pontil, and the untidy ends of the canes are visible, which rather lets the piece down.

Magnum Seven Row Concentric. Height 2". Dia. 4.2". $500-600. ***Courtesy of Dr. Geoffrey Dutton.***

Another very precise set-up, probably from the same factory as the previous weight. Again a very well made centre cane in the Bacchus style with the red centre being encased in a tube of white glass. The pastel shades are also Bacchus features. The canes are complex ruffles and the whole piece is extremely well done.

Base of Magnum Seven Row Concentric.

The base shows the outside layer of blue canes all squashed together to form a solid ring of blue, almost like a torsade. This powder blue coloring is very unusual and only very rarely seen in an English weight.

Seven Row Concentric. Height 1.9". Dia. 2.9". $500-600. ***Courtesy of Bill Volkman.***

This example, with the powder blue outer row of canes, has open and ruffle canes that suggest it is from the Bacchus factory; it may be an early weight from this glassworks. It has a perfectly flat base with a rough pontil mark

Seven Row Concentric. Height 2.1". Dia. 3.1". $700-900. ***Courtesy of Bill Volkman.***

This paperweight has mixed simple and complex ruffles canes in soft pastel shades, including the pistachio green canes that are so reminiscent of the Bacchus colors. Many of these unknown weights are more than likely to be from the Bacchus glassworks, but all have something or other that does not seem quite right. In this weight, the base has a rough pontil mark and the cane ends all finish very neatly on the edge of the weight. It also has a deep ridge where the set-up has been joined to the crown, a feature that so distinguishes the modern Whitefriars paperweights, but the central feature cane is undeniably Bacchus. This weight is too good to be one of the first that Bacchus produced, but does not quite have all the finer qualities of their later weights.

Close Packed Millefiori with Five Head Silhouettes. Height 2". Dia. 3.3". $750-900. ***Courtesy of Bill Volkman.***

This close pack has a garland of ruffle canes holding the canes together. These ruffles are very similar to those made by Bacchus. The many varied canes in this interesting weight include powder blue cross canes in white tubes (another Bacchus feature) and five off white head canes that look male rather than the well known Victoria Silhouettes. Once again I am inclined to place this weight in the early Bacchus category.

Detail View of Close Packed Millefiori.

The enlarged view shows many canes that are very similar to the well known Bacchus canes, although some have slight differences.

Five Row Concentric with Twenty-Nine Victoria Silhouette Canes. Height 1.8". Dia. 2.5". $1200-1500. ***Courtesy of Bill Volkman.***

These canes all seem to be from the Bacchus glassworks and the weight may be an early piece, but the small size and deep ridge mark on the almost flat base suggests it was made elsewhere. The cane ends are finished neatly on the edge of the paperweight, which also has a rough pontil mark. This and several other weights that are of this quality suggest that they were the start of the quality era in the Bacchus production. Or is it possible that another Birmingham glassworks was also making paperweights, buying and using Bacchus canes?

Four Row Concentric. Height 1.8". Dia. 2.9". $600-700. *Courtesy of Bill Volkman.*

Pure white ruffle canes and a cog with a large white centre may be an aid to the identification of this fine paperweight. The central pastry mould cane suggests that a Bacchus attribution would be in order.

Close Packed Millefiori. Height 2.2". Dia. 3.5". $300-500. *Courtesy of Bill Volkman.*

At first glance this seemingly innocuous and pallid close pack offers the collector very little interest. The centre cog cane stands out like a beacon of light in a very drab background of cog and tube canes, but on closer inspection a small red tube cane on the inner row has a Victoria Head Silhouette cane buried inside, only just visible without a magnifying glass because of the gray colored glass used to make the head.

Base of Five Row Concentric with Twenty-Nine Victoria Silhouette Canes.

The base clearly shows the deep ridge mark and rough pontil. The cane ends are finished by turning under the weight rather than drawn in to the centre of the base as with the majority of the Bacchus weights. Whoever made this paperweight, still made a fine weight.

Four Row Concentric. Height 1.8". Dia. 2.9". $500-700. *Courtesy of Bill Volkman.*

The central pastry mould cane looks as though it was made by Bacchus, as it would seem that they were the only glassworks to encase the central feature cane in this heavy band of white glass. Many unknown paperweights have features that link them to certain glass houses, like this centre cane, but we must not forget that the experimental period in paperweight production by a glasshouse must have been quite substantial. It may be that a company such as Bacchus experimented for many years before they had the necessary skills in place to proceed to a production run. The workers were encouraged by the management at many glasshouses to try their hand at new ideas and techniques, usually after the work shift had ended and if sufficient glass was left over from the day's production. Once again this weight has several non-Bacchus features, including an inverted foot and ridge mark. This piece has a rough pontil, but the cane ends are finished very neatly around the edge of the weight.

Bacchus Five Row Concentric, c. 1850. Height 2". Dia. 3". $2000-2500. *Courtesy of Bill Volkman.*

This piece and the Bacchus paperweight below left have been included in this section to allow comparisons of canes to be made. This weight has a ridge mark on the base which is hollow ground. The outer row of canes have been drawn down and under to the centre of the base.

Bacchus Magnum Five Row Concentric, c. 1850. Height 2.75". Dia. 4.1". $3000-3500. *Courtesy of Bill Volkman.*

This Bacchus weight has the same central feature cane as the example above it, except that this one has an extra ruffle included and is not so heavily encased and is just a variation. This weight also has a concave base, rough pontil mark, striations in the glass, and a ridge mark on the base. An early weight from Bacchus, still in the experimental stages.

Five Row Concentric. Height 2.3". Dia. 3.2". $600-800. *Courtesy of Bill Volkman.*

A fine blue and white concentric weight that almost became a carpet ground. All the canes are encased in white tubes, Bacchus style.

Four Row Concentric. $250-350. *Courtesy of Bill* Volkman

A combination of simple cogs and solid rods around a large centre cane.

Profile of Four Row Concentric.

This weight has the added attraction of a well finished and unusual base. The canes are drawn down to the centre of the base where the pontil rod has been removed; the weight has then been encased further to add extra glass to the base. This is the first weight I have seen with this feature and was possibly an experimental piece.

Six Row Concentric. Height 2.2". Dia. 3.4". $250-350. *Author's Collection.*

A row of blue and white ruffle canes sits next to an encased red cross in a cog cane. Three other rows of cross canes can be seen. The base is concave with a rough pontil mark.

Four Row Concentric Basket. $350-500. *Courtesy of Bill Volkman.*

This is an unusual weight with the outer row of powder blue canes pulled together to make a solid torsade. The outer row has then been pulled downwards to make a very good basket.

Profile of Four Row Concentric Basket.

Although the canes in this paperweight are very ordinary, the basket makes this weight very rare and collectible. This was probably an experimental piece as I have found it to be unique in design among English weights. The whole process has been extremely well executed.

Endnotes

Chapter Four

[1]*Glass Paperweights of the Bergstrom Mahler Museum*. United States Historical Society Press.

[2] Kulles, George N. *Identifying Antique Paperweights (Millefiori)*. Santa Cruz, California: Paperweight Press, 1985.

Chapter Ten

[1]Andrews, Frank. *Ysart Glass*. Volo Edition, London.

Glossary

The following are some of the commonly used terms relating to paperweights.

Air Bubbles. Silvery air bubbles can be added to the inside of a paperweight, as seen in a dump weight, by piercing the still soft glass with a sharp steel pin or steel comb. This traps a small amount of air inside, and when the pin is withdrawn, closing the hole, the trapped air will expand on reheating the glass.

Annealing. All paperweights and glass articles must be cooled very slowly, the time depending on the mass of the article concerned. A paperweight would be left in a slowly cooling oven for approximately twenty-four hours. This slow cooling process prevents cracking of the glass.

Baccarat, French Glasshouse. Perhaps the most famous of paperweight makers in the nineteenth century, still producing quality paperweights and millefiori objects today.

Basal Ring. This refers to that part of the paperweight base which touches the surface that the paperweight is resting on. When a paperweight has its pontil mark removed by grinding, a shallow depression is formed which usually extends outwards towards the edge, leaving a flat area of approximately 0.25 inches to rest upon. This prevents scratching and obscuring the canework beneath the paperweight.

Basket. A basket describes the outer row of canes drawn down and beneath the paperweight, enclosing the bottom half of the weight.

Bohemia. An area that includes Czechoslovakia and much of Eastern Europe which produced glassware and paperweights in the "classic period."

Button. "On the button" is a term used to describe the set-up of canes after they have been removed from the steel or iron mould. Although not much bigger than an actual button, the magnifying property of the glass dome on a paperweight enlarges the button to make it fill out the weight.

Canes. The basic element in the majority of paperweights. Pliable glass of a single color is drawn out by two glassworkers attaching a pontil rod on either end of a lump of glass approximately 3 inches in diameter and 6 inches long. The workers then move away from each other, holding the glass 3 feet above the floor. As the glass is pulled in two directions, the centre reduces down to approximately 0.25 inches and cools. The cane continues to be drawn out to 40 or 50 feet in length. After 30 seconds, to allow cooling, the rod is laid on the floor and cut into 1 foot lengths with pincers.

Carpet Ground. This description applies when the same canes are used to cover the bottom element of the paperweight; usually other, more colorful canes, will then be set into this "carpet."

Classic Period. Any paperweights described as from "the classic period" means they were made from around 1845 to 1852. This was the height of the English and French paperweight popularity, when most of the quality pieces were made.

Clichy, French Glasshouse. A major producer of superior quality paperweights in the nineteenth century.

Close Packed. Canes bundled together and held in no particular order or pattern before being encased in the final covering of glass.

Cog Cane. This can be a simple one color rod, formed in a serrated mould, and may be the base for a more complex cane.

Complex Cane. This is a combination of many smaller rods and canes, as many as one hundred bundled together, reheated and drawn out to miniaturize the cane to normal size. A magnifying glass is then required to appreciate its complexity.

Concentric. The majority of English paperweights were "concentrics." From a central large cane, rings of ever increasing circles of millefiori canes reach out to the edge of the weight. There are usually five or six rows, but as many as eight rows can been found.

Cushion. The canes are set in rings of metal before being picked up by the soft glass on the end of a pontil rod. This gives the appearance of a pin cushion.

Dipping. This was a method of covering and adding a further layer of colored or clear glass. The object was dipped in the required color to pick up just enough to cover the top; this added glass was then pulled and pushed all over the object with the worker's pliers and tweezer type tools to create a thin layer of a different color. The object is then reheated and smoothed off. Further coats can then be added.

Dump or Doorstop. This type of green glass weight was usually made at the end of the day's workings, to use up any leftover glass. They were mainly made by the glasshouses producing bottles, but practically every glasshouse made them. The quality was such that the pieces were only suitable for holding open the door.

Facet. Many weights were cut on the sides and top to allow the viewer an unobstructed view of the internal motif. This could be a flat or concave cut of approximately 1 inch.

Flash. This is a thin layer of colored glass sometimes applied all over or just to the base of a weight. If applied all over, windows are normally cut to allow viewing inside the weight, as with an overlay weight.

Foot. Paperweights and inkwells have this feature to break up the outline. The foot is created by applied pressure with a pair of steel tongs while the glass is still soft.

Frigger. Friggers are pieces of work made by the glassworkers with and without the knowledge of the management. The purpose could be to use up waste glass, expand on skills and new techniques, or to use as gifts for family and friends.

Gather. A gather of glass is a lump of molten glass taken from the furnace and used to form another part of the paperweight, such as the dome.

Intaglio. This is a method of producing an image that looks to be on the inside of a glass paperweight. The image is produced by pressing hot soft glass onto a sculpted form, which leaves its impression in the glass. By applying acid to leave the glass matt on the impressed surface, the resulting image can be viewed through the dome of the clear glass.

Latticinio or Lace. Normal diameter rods with spiral twists of white or colored threads, with the length being longer than the diameter, sometimes used as a base on which other millefiori canes are set.

Lampwork. This is the method used to create flowers and other worked items, using a small gas or other fueled torch. With a fine hot flame, glass can be worked into any shape imaginable.

Magnum. This refers to the size given to a paperweight that is of a larger diameter than normal, usually over 3.75 inches.

Marver Plate. This is a solid steel plate used by the glassworkers to roll out and shape the soft glass. It is on this plate that the glass can become contaminated with dust and dirt, and although not seen while the glass is in this semi molten stage, particles of dirt show up in a magnified version when the paperweight is cold.

Millefiori. Originating in Italy, millefiori means a "thousand flowers," as most millefiori canes are said to look like flower heads. Millefiori canes were first used in glass from the second century AD

Overlay. The paperweight can be dipped into colored glass after its final covering of clear glass. This outer layer can then be cut with windows to allow the insides to be seen.

Pastry Mould Cane. This cane is usually deeply serrated, with the bottom being flared out larger than the top, as with a ladies skirt.

Pontil Rod and Mark. This is a steel rod that can be hollow to allow air to be blown through in order to expand the glass in size, and to gather the glass from the furnace. The paperweight is formed and worked while attached to this rod. When the weight is ready to be detached from the pontil rod, air is gently blown on the stem of glass attached to the paperweight. This cooling allows the glassworker to tap the rod sharply, leading the finished paperweight to fall into a soft, flame-resistant material, after which it is taken immediately to the annealing oven. When cool and annealed, the rough mark where the weight was attached to the rod is removed by grinding. Many glasshouses never removed this mark if it did not protrude below the base of the weight.

Ridge mark. When the cane set-up is picked up from the steel or iron mould by a gather of glass, the two halves stick together and usually leave an indentation where they meet. This is quite common on English paperweights.

Saint Louis. A notable French Glasshouse which produced paperweights and related glassware in the "classic period," especially fine concentrics.

Set-ups. This describes the millefiori canes that have been cut to the desired lengths (usually about 0.25 inches), which are then sorted into size and design, and, with the help of tweezers, placed into a steel or iron ring with a base. The designs are set in concentric circles, starting from the outside edge, with ever decreasing circles towards the centre, where a much larger cane will usually be used to centralize the set-up.

Silhouette Cane. Heads and animals are the usual subjects in these canes that are viewed in cross section after they are moulded, drawn out, and cut.

Spaced Millefiori. A type in which canes are placed in the paperweight in a non-geometric pattern but with spaces between them.

Striae. This word is used to describe the stress lines that can sometimes be seen in glass paperweights. The almost transparent lines are caused by the near molten glass being twisted and turned in the working process. Occasionally these lines are on the surface, being caused by pressure on the dome from the tools used to smooth and shape the final gather of glass. They can be felt with the tips of the fingers, feeling like slight ripples, and can cause distortion to the motif inside the weight. They can be polished out if on the surface, however nothing can be done with lines that are internal.

Sulphide. A moulded ceramic glass paste portrait of a famous person which is encased in a gather of glass to form a paperweight or used for decorating other objects.

Torsade. A twisted cane that normally encircles the bottom of a paperweight like a rope.

Bibliography and Recomended Reading

To further your knowledge of English paperweights in general, I highly recommend the following books.

Hollister, Paul Jr. *The Encyclopedia of Glass Paperweights.* Santa Cruz, California: Paperweight Press, 1969.

Kulles, George N. *Identifying Antique Paperweights, (Millefiori).* Santa Cruz, California: Paperweight Press, 1985.

Jargstorf, Sibylle. *Paperweights.* West Chester, Pennsylvania: Schiffer Publishing Ltd., 1991.

Mackay, James. *Glass Paperweights.* London: Ward Lock Ltd., 1973.

Notes